Ethical Decision Making

Ethical Decision Making

A Guide for Counselors in the 21st Century

Richard D. Parsons, Ph.D., and Peter J. Boccone, Ph.D.

Bassim Hamadeh, CEO and Publisher
Amy Smith, Senior Project Editor
Abbey Hastings, Associate Production Editor
Emely Villavicencio, Senior Graphic Designer
Stephanie Kohl, Licensing Coordinator
Natalie Piccotti, Director of Marketing
Kassie Graves, Vice President of Editorial
Jamie Giganti, Director of Academic Publishing

Copyright © 2021 by Cognella, Inc. All rights reserved. No part of this publication may be reprinted, reproduced, transmitted, or utilized in any form or by any electronic, mechanical, or other means, now known or hereafter invented, including photocopying, microfilming, and recording, or in any information retrieval system without the written permission of Cognella, Inc. For inquiries regarding permissions, translations, foreign rights, audio rights, and any other forms of reproduction, please contact the Cognella Licensing Department at rights@cognella.com.

Trademark Notice: Product or corporate names may be trademarks or registered trademarks and are used only for identification and explanation without intent to infringe.

Cover image: Copyright © 2018 iStockphoto LP/akinbostanci.

To those individuals who have served as models of ethical behavior,
Dr. Emmanuel Ahia, Dr. Robert Wicks, Conrad Parsons, and the students who
remind us of why we do what we do.

Brief Contents

Preface   xv

Acknowledgments   xvii

Section I: Beyond Understanding to Applying   1

1. The What and Why of Professional Codes of Ethics   3
2. Ethics in Counseling: Navigating the Gray   15
3. Models to Guide Ethical Decision Making   25

Section II: 21st-Century Challenges to Ethical Practice   41

4. Practice in a Diverse World   43
5. Client and Context   57
6. Boundaries   67
7. Counseling Beyond the Office Walls (Distance Counseling)   81
8. From One to Many: Couples and Families   93
9. Evidence-Based Treatment and Practice   109
10. Conflicts: Ethics and the Law   123

Index   131

About the Authors   135

Detailed Contents

Preface   xv

Acknowledgments   xvii

Section I: Beyond Understanding to Applying   1

1   The What and Why of Professional Codes of Ethics   3
    Codes: A Mark of a Profession   3
        Codes of Ethics—"Living"/Evolving   4
    Reflection of Values   5
    Beyond Knowing Ethics to Living Ethically   5
        Values to Principles   6
    Practical and Legal   9
        Codes of Ethics: Practical and Useful   9
        Ethical Codes and Their Legal Connection   10
    Additional Resources   12
        Print-Based   12
        Web-Based   12
    References   12

2   Ethics in Counseling: Navigating the Gray   15
    Ethics: A Guide Versus a Definitive Mandate   15
        Absolutism Versus Relativism   16
        Utilitarianism Versus Deontology   18
    Principle Ethics   19
    Ethical Codes   19
        The Purpose of Ethical Codes   20
        The Structure of Ethical Codes   20
        Mandatory Ethical Codes   20
        Discretionary Ethical Codes   21
        Multiple Ethical Codes   22
    Additional Resources   23
        Print-Based   23
        Web-Based   23
    References   23

3   Models to Guide Ethical Decision Making   25
    Practice-Based Models   26
    Integrative Model   29
    The Transcultural Integrative Model   30
    Counselor Value-Based Conflict Model   33
    A Practical, Culturally Sensitive Model for Ethical Decision Making   33
        Step 1: Preparing for Ethical Practice   34
        Step 2: Identifying the Problem   34
        Step 3: Formulating the Ethical Concern   34
        Step 4: Determining of the Nature and Dimensions of the Dilemma   35
        Step 5: Generating Potential Courses of Action   35
        Step 6: Assessing Options   35
        Step 7: Selecting and Implementing a Course of Action   35
        Step 8: Documenting the Steps Taken   36
    Additional Resources   39
        Print-Based   39
        Web-Based   39
    References   39

Section II: 21st-Century Challenges to Ethical Practice   41

4   Practice in a Diverse World   43
    A Challenge to Our Professional Assumptions   44
    Sensitivity to Diversity and Minority Experience   44
        Diversity and the Counseling Relationship   45
        Assessment, Diagnosis, and Problem Identification   46
        Intervention and Treatment Planning   47
    Multicultural Competency: An Ethical "Given"   48
    A Transcultural Approach to Ethical Decision Making   49
    Applying an Ethical Decision-Making Model   50
        The Dilemma   50
        Identifying the Problem   50
        Formulating the Ethical Concern   51
        Generating Potential Courses of Action   51
        Consulting With a Colleague?   51
        Assessing Each Option   52
        Selecting a Course of Action   52
        Implementing a Course of Action   52
    Additional Resources   53
        Print-Based   53
        Web-Based   53
    References   54

5 Client and Context — 57

- Client Served 57
  - Minors 58
  - When Competence Is Challenged 60
  - Mandated Clients 61
- Context and Setting 62
- Additional Resources 64
  - Print-Based 64
  - Web-Based 64
- References 65

6 Boundaries — 67

- Boundaries—What and Why 67
- Boundaries—Dynamic 68
  - Boundary Violation 69
  - Boundary Crossing 70
  - A Slippery Slope? 72
- Boundary Challenges in the 21st Century 73
  - Social Media and "Friending" 74
  - Email and Texting 74
- Applying an Ethical Decision-Making Model 75
  - The Dilemma 75
  - Identifying the Problem 76
  - Formulating the Ethical Concern 76
  - Generating Potential Courses of Action 77
  - Consulting with a Colleague? 77
  - Assessing Each Option 77
  - Selecting a Course of Action 77
  - Implementing a Course of Action 78
- Additional Resources 79
  - Print-Based 79
  - Web-Based 79
- References 79

7 Counseling Beyond the Office Walls (Distance Counseling) — 81

- Distance Counseling on the Rise 82
- Distance Counseling and the Law 83
  - Interstate Practice 83
- Distance Counseling and Ethics 84
  - Knowledge 84
  - Informed Consent and Security 84
  - Distance Counseling Relationship 87
- Applying an Ethical Decision-Making Model 88
  - The Dilemma 88
  - Identifying the Problem 88
  - Formulating the Ethical Concern 89

        Generating Potential Courses of Action   89
        Consulting With a Colleague?   90
        Assessing Each Option   90
        Selecting a Course of Action   90
        Implementing a Course of Action   90
    Additional Resources   91
        Print-Based   91
        Web-Based   92
    References   92

8   From One to Many: Couples and Families   93
    Special Competence: Not Simply Individual Counseling, Times Two   94
    Informed Consent   96
    Boundaries and the Avoidance of Siding   97
    Confidentiality: Sharing What, With Whom   99
        Records Access   99
        Privileged Communications   101
    Applying an Ethical Decision-Making Model   101
        The Dilemma   102
        Identifying the Problem   102
        Formulating the Ethical Concern   103
        Generating Potential Courses of Action   104
        Consulting With a Colleague?   104
        Assessing Each Option   104
        Selecting a Course of Action   104
        Implementing a Course of Action   105
    Additional Resources   106
        Print-Based   106
        Web-Based   106
    References   106

9   Evidence-Based Treatment and Practice   109
    Evidence-Based Practice   109
    Treatment Selection   111
    Issue of Competence   113
    When Scientific Foundation Is Unavailable   114
    Applying an Ethical Decision-Making Model   116
        The Dilemma   116
        Identifying the Problem   116
        Formulating the Ethical Concern   117
        Generating Potential Courses of Action   117
        Consulting With a Colleague?   117
        Assessing Each Option   117
        Selecting a Course of Action   118
        Implementing a Course of Action   118

Additional Resources   120
　　　　　Print-Based   120
　　　　　Web-Based   120
　　　References   120

10　Conflicts: Ethics and the Law　　　　　　　　　　　　　　　123
　　　A Force of Nature   123
　　　　　The Nature of Counseling Ethics and Law   124
　　　Law Versus Ethics   125
　　　Navigating Legal and Ethical Conflicts   126
　　　Additional Resources   128
　　　　　Print-Based   128
　　　　　Web-Based   128
　　　References   128

Index　　　　　　　　　　　　　　　　　　　　　　　　　　　　131

About the Authors　　　　　　　　　　　　　　　　　　　　　　135

Preface

I looked at the code, and I'm still not sure what to do.

While the comment that opens this section was made by a first-year mental health counselor working in a rural crisis center, it is an experience that has been shared by many professional counselors. Ours is a profession that invites us to step into the often less than clean and clear-cut experience of the counseling dynamic. It is this dynamic nature of counseling that often brings ethical challenge and the need for ethical decisions.

Referring to a professional code of ethics will undoubtedly provide some guidance at these times of practice decision making, but the emphasis is on "some." Codes of ethics are not clear directives, nor are they templates or formulas for action. They are guidelines that need to be adjusted and tailored to the uniqueness of each counseling relationship. The process of navigating the circumstances of a counseling relationship in order to engage in practices that are both effective and ethical is complex. It is the process of ethical decision making and the application of the professional code of ethics that serves as the focus of this text.

More Than Understanding

The need for all counselors to be educated in the standards and codes of professional ethics is a given. To this end, numerous texts have been created to describe, explain, and illustrate the specific ethical principles guiding the practice of counseling.

There is abundant evidence, both research and anecdotal, that illustrates that while the understanding of the codes of conduct is core to professional training, this comprehension alone is insufficient to guarantee these principles will be lived out in practice. The frequency of ethical violations highlights the fact that knowledge sometimes fails to take form in action.

Translating the "the principle printed on the page" to the "at-the-moment clinical decision" is difficult. Counseling decisions are not always, if ever, truly black or white. Issues presented within the counseling dynamic do not fit neatly into an ethical box or concern, and their complexity can try even the most seasoned practitioner. To respond ethically, with consistency, is nearly impossible in the absence of a structure or scaffold to guide that decision.

The current text provides just such a structure or model to guide the ethical decision making of counselors in the 21st century. The chapters in Section I provide an overview of the need and challenge for ethical practice and provide an introduction to models of ethical decision making. Section II highlights the unique opportunities and challenges that counselors will encounter working in a time of expanded diversity and increasing technology. Chapters in Section II provide illustrations of the application of an ethical decision-making model to specific ethical dilemmas.

About the Format of This Book

Each chapter opens with a counselor's reflection. These opening reflections are used to set the stage for the content that follows. It may be helpful to return to these opening vignettes following completion of the chapter, applying what has been learned in the chapter to that scenario. Also, each chapter will provide case illustrations and guided exercises designed to make the concepts discussed come alive.

This text, like all texts, provides an expanded knowledge base and guidance in the development of additional skills. Knowledge and skill alone are of limited value unless applied. We hope that the material presented facilitates the readers' ability to recognize the many ethical challenges presented within any counseling relationship and to effectively employ an ethical decision-making model to guide their practice at these moments.

Acknowledgments

While the title page of this text identifies Richard Parsons and Peter Boccone as authors, the truth is that numerous individuals have helped craft this book through their valued suggestions and support. The book has been enriched by the careful review and recommendations offered by Perry C. Francis (Eastern Michigan University), Caroline S. Booth (North Carolina A&T State University), Hassiem Ayele Kamubi (Florida Agricultural and Mechanical University), and Rachel Vannatta (Immaculata University). We would like to also acknowledge the outstanding support provided by the people at Cognella Academic Publishing, including Abbey Hastings, Associate Production Editor, Carrie Montoya, manager of revisions and author care, and Amy Smith, our project editor, who certainly kept us on schedule. Finally, a special thank-you, as always, goes to Kassie Graves, who remains a mentor, an advocate, and most importantly, a friend.

Beyond Understanding to Applying

1

Chapter 1

The What and Why of Professional Codes of Ethics

I began to feel like a professional when I took my ethics course.

IT MAY HAPPEN during your first theories class or field experience. It may happen the day of graduation or the first day on the job. Regardless of when or where, there is a moment when the realization that one is no longer a student but is now a professional "hits" us all. For the counselor quoted at the beginning of the chapter, that experience occurred during a course on professional ethics.

This is not surprising, given the fact that our profession's code of ethics has a long, rich history—one pointing to the evolution of counseling as a profession. It is not surprising in that understanding our code of ethics awakens us to the underlying values and perspective that we, as counselors, employ when engaging in our practice. It is not surprising in that understanding our professional code of conduct also invites us to understand the complexity of the human condition and the responsibilities we, serving in our professional role, bear in serving those in need.

Our code of ethics is the mantle of our professionalism. The value of a code of ethics to the profession and the professional serves as the focus of this chapter. After completing this chapter, readers will be able to

1. explain the relationship between values, principles, and codes of ethics;
2. describe the values supporting the American Counseling Association's code of ethics;
3. describe the value of a code of ethics to the profession and the professional; and
4. explain the nature of the relationship between the code of ethics and the law.

Codes: A Mark of a Profession

A defining characteristic of a professional organization is the formulation of a code or system of standards (Gorman & Sandefur, 2011). The establishment of a code of ethics signifies the maturation of a profession and results from the evolution of a collective professional identity within the organization (Mabe & Rollin, 1986).

A code of ethics clarifies an organization's mission, values, and principles and links these with standards of professional practice. Written codes of conduct or ethics can become benchmarks against which individual and organizational performance can be measured.

A code of ethics, regardless of the profession, provides a structure for the articulation of norms and expectations for practitioners. It serves as a benchmark against which the performance of the individual and the organization as a whole can be assessed. For those engaged as professional counselors, our code of ethics serves as a collective statement of steps to be taken to protect clients from harm (Welfel, 2010). It is a framework established to ensure integrity and responsibility on the part of the counselor.

Codes of Ethics—"Living"/Evolving

Professional codes of ethics are dynamic documents, modified and adapted as society and professions change. Professional codes of ethics are responsive to changing societal mores as well as the expanding and changing demands placed on the professional. While codes of ethics for those engaged in the mental health field are relatively recent developments (Neukrug, 2000), their creation has a rich history in the medical profession.

The medical profession has served as the model for the ongoing development and articulation of a professional code of conduct. It could be argued that the Hippocratic oath, having been written in the 5th century B.C.E., is one of the oldest directives for professional practice (Riddick, 2003). In the oath, the physician pledges to prescribe only beneficial treatment and to refrain from causing harm. In addition, the oath calls for practitioners—in this case, physicians—to live an exemplary personal and professional life. The first modern code of medical ethics was developed by Thomas Percival, an English physician, in 1794, and a later expansion (1803) introduced the term "medical ethics" (Pettifor, 2001).

Psychology's foray into the formulation of formal regulations of practice and the development of a code of ethics appeared in 1953 (American Psychological Association [APA], 1953). This code was in part a reaction to the atrocities of the many medical and psychological experiments that occurred during World War II (Sinclair et al., 1996).

A similar code of conduct for counselors remained wanting for a number of years, with the first code appearing in the early 1960s. The American Personnel and Guidance Association (APGA), a precursor to today's American Counseling Association, produced its first standard and code of ethical conduct in 1961. Through numerous iterations of both organizational name and code, the APGA evolved into the American Counseling Association (ACA) and produced the first code under the ACA banner in 1988. As a "living" document that is responsive to the changes, nature, and needs of our consumers, the ACA code has evolved through revisions in 1995 and 2005 that have resulted in its current formulation (ACA, 2014).

Reflection of Values

A code of conduct and ethical practice is more than a template guiding practice decisions. Our code of ethics reflects the values and moral principles collectively owned and espoused by the members of our profession. It is a system of principles that gives form to the values that support our professional practice and research.

As noted by Neukrug (2000), "ethical guidelines are moral, not legal, documents" (p. 49). In this framework, it becomes clear that it is not sufficient for counselors to simply know the code of ethics or even attempt to follow the structure when engaging their profession—the code "calls" us to embrace, at both a professional and personal level, the values that have taken form in the specifics of the codes. Doing so is a process; a journey in which we identify our biases, explore our own beliefs and how they develop, and understand how those fit or do not fit in our role as a counselor. As professional counselors we assume fiduciary obligation with our clients; that is, we embrace "special duty to care for the welfare of one's clients or patients" (Haas & Malouf, 1995, p. 2). Therefore, our standard, relative to moral principles, is higher than that of the layperson.

While the code of ethics does not subvert the individual counselor's personal needs and values, it does place the needs and interests of the client in the forefront (DeMitchell et al., 2013; Gorman & Sandefur, 2011). Our code calls us to (a) embrace the inherent worth and dignity of each client; (b) respect each client's uniqueness, autonomy, and right to self-determination; (c) honor human growth and development; and (d) respect the diversity within our clientele. These are values that inform the principles underlying our code of ethics. They represent an essential way of expressing a general ethical commitment that becomes more precisely defined and action oriented when expressed as a principle, such as, *"The primary responsibility of counselors is to respect the dignity and promote the welfare of clients"* (ACA 2014, Standard A.1.a).

Beyond Knowing Ethics to Living Ethically

The preamble of the code of ethics (ACA, 2014) makes it clear that the standards are not intended to be depersonalized "suggestions" for professional practice. As noted in the preamble, the code of ethics reflects the core values of the profession, values which are "an important way of living out an ethical commitment."

While the code of ethics is prescriptive in terms of the professional behavior expected, the true hope of our profession is that each counselor will internalize the profession's collective values and articulated principles. The implication of the phrase "living out" is that it is not sufficient to merely step into the code of ethics at times of practice decisions; instead, we as professional counselors need to embrace the underlying values and fundamental principles as personal, as well as professional, ways of living ethically.

Exercise 1.1 provides a listing of the core professional values identified by the ACA (2014) in the code's preamble. You are invited to reflect on each of the stated values and how they relate to both your personal life and professional life.

EXERCISE 1.1

Directions: The following chart provides a listing of the core professional values of the counseling profession (ACA, 2014, preamble). The wording has been adapted so that the values can be applied in both personal and professional life. Review each one. Spend time reflecting on the words and their implication, not just for your practice but also for your worldview and life choices.

Identify how the value is evident in your personal life. Similarly, identify where in your professional experience you may have given evidence of this value, or where and how you could see that value directing your practice decision. The challenge is to develop from knowing these values to owning these values continually.

Values	Evidence in Personal Life	Ways to Embody as a Professional
Enhancing human development throughout the life span		
Honoring diversity in support of the worth, dignity, potential, and uniqueness of people within their social and cultural contexts		
Promoting social justice		
Safeguarding the integrity of relationships		
Addressing tasks in a competent and ethical manner		

Values to Principles

The distinction between values and principles was conceptualized in the 18th-century writings of Jeremy Bentham. For Bentham (1948), whereas values articulate "an aspiration of an ideal moral state," a principle was "a general law or rule that guides behaviour or decisions" (p. 2). Table 1.1 lists the principles that emerge from our professional values and that in turn serve as a foundation for our code of ethics. With the articulation of principles, we begin to

TABLE 1.1. PRINCIPLES UNDERGIRDING OUR CODE OF ETHICS

Principle	Counselor Embodiment	Illustration of Decision Guided by Principle
Autonomy: respect for the client's right to be self-governing	A counselor who embraces this principle will engage in activities such as providing information essential to informed consent, protecting confidentiality, and contracting in advance of any commitment by the client. The counselor emphasizes the voluntary nature of the client's participation and avoids any form of client manipulation against their will.	A counselor working with minors takes time to explain in a language suitable for the developmental level of the client the elements of counseling, including the rights and limits to privacy, in order to obtain the client's "informed assent."
Beneficence: a commitment to promoting the client's well-being	With this principle as a guide, a counselor systematically monitors practice and outcome to ensure that counseling is unfolding in the best interest of the client.	In working with a client, a counselor becomes aware that the nature of the "real" issue (versus the presenting concern) is beyond the limits of their competence and therefore assists the client with a referral to a counselor with the needed competency.
Nonmaleficence: a commitment to avoiding harm to the client	This principle is seen in a counselor's action targeting the prevention of client exploitation (e.g., boundary setting and maintenance) and/or of practicing when impaired and unable to provide ethical, effective service.	A counselor who recognizes the limits to their physical energy and ability to fully attend to clients late in the evening modifies their schedule to see clients until 5:00 p.m. and no later.
Justice: the fair and impartial treatment of all clients and the provision of adequate services	In embracing justice as a principle guiding practice, a counselor is mindful of engaging time and resources impartially among all clients. The counselor appreciates differences among clients and is committed to equality of service.	A school counselor is mindful of the students who not only enjoy but positively contribute to the lunch-bunch sessions held at school. The counselor implements a plan to ensure that all of the students in their charge would have the opportunity to attend lunch-bunch sessions.

Principle	Counselor Embodiment	Illustration of Decision Guided by Principle
Fidelity: the act of honoring commitments and keeping promises, including fulfilling one's responsibilities of trust in professional relationships	Fidelity involves faithfulness and the honoring of commitments, be that to the time of an appointment or something more involved like the maintenance of confidentiality.	Working as part of an EAP team, a counselor, as agreed on in the initial therapeutic contract, provides the client with weekly summary reports that the counselor, in turn, provides their supervisor.
Veracity: the act of dealing truthfully with individuals with whom counselors come into professional contact	Veracity is a principle that will often take shape in the process of gaining informed consent, with a counselor providing honest, accurate information about issues such as billing, office policies, professional background, limits to confidentiality, and treatment approach. Veracity also guides the disclosure of information to the client about their test results or diagnostic profile.	Having completed the analyses of the diagnostic testing, a counselor provides accurate, developmentally appropriate interpretation of the data to the client. While being sensitive to the language employed, choosing that which was accurate and understandable to a nonprofessional, the counselor was sure not to omit or deliberately withhold relevant and potentially helpful information.

operationalize the values that should guide our practice decisions. Table 1.1 also provides illustrations of how these principles may be called into practice.

It would be comforting to state that all situations encountered in practice will be strongly supported by one or more of these principles without conflict or contradiction. As you will soon discover or may have already experienced, there are times when one must abandon the desire to reconcile all applicable principles in favor of choosing the principle or principles that offer the best chance of making an ethical decision. Case Illustration 1.1 provides a simple illustration of just such a dilemma.

CASE ILLUSTRATION 1.1

MS. TAYLOR AND RACHEL

The counselor, Ms. Taylor, recently took a job with a community mental health agency serving a midwestern rural community. The center had three satellite offices spanning a 60-mile area, each employing one therapist. Ms. Taylor was a licensed professional counselor and active member of both the ACA and the American Association of Pastoral Counselors. Ms. Taylor was, according to her previous employer, a highly competent professional who "felt called to the profession" and "approached her clients with genuine care and concern."

Rachel, the client, was self-referred and came to counseling because of intense anxiety and depression. Rachel shared that she had recently come to grips with being a lesbian but felt conflicted, given her family values. In the process of intake, Ms. Taylor became aware of her own conflict. Although concerned about Rachel's struggle, Ms. Taylor was aware that her values and religious beliefs were being called into conflict.

She experienced concern about her ability to develop and engage in a nonjudgmental, unconditionally valuing working alliance and as a result was fearful that she might violate the professional value of non-maleficence. She also realized that refusing to see this client would be a violation of the justice value and recognized the harm that could occur as a result of a refusal to treat. As an extension to her standard sharing of information for informed consent, she shared her concerns about being able to keep her values out of the interaction. She invited Rachel to consider the options of attempting to work together or engaging another counselor (the closest of which was 20 miles from Rachel's home). Ms. Taylor thus supported the client's autonomy by inviting Rachel to decide as to location and therapist. She also shared that if Rachel would like to continue, that she (Ms. Taylor) would, with Rachel's consent, engage in supervision around their work.

FOR REFLECTION AND DISCUSSION

1. As noted in the illustration, "Ms. Taylor was aware that her values and religious beliefs were being called into conflict," specifically as it applied to Rachel's sexual orientation. Assume you are Ms. Taylor's supervisor. What would you suggest? Is it as simple as putting one's values aside?
2. Should Ms. Taylor inform Rachel about her felt conflict? Is this data important in order for Rachel to provide informed consent to continue in counseling with Ms. Taylor?

Practical and Legal

Viewed as aspirational, our professional ethics shine a light on the values and principles that we are all invited to embrace and embody. Beyond such an aspirational goal, our code of ethics serves a very practical purpose.

Codes of Ethics: Practical and Useful

While calling each of us to higher, loftier goals, our code of ethics serves a number of very practical ends. Our code of ethics serves as a guide, a scaffold for ethical and effective practice. It is an articulation of unacceptable behaviors and as such is a framework to be used when carrying out one's professional responsibilities.

Banks (2001) studied the codes of ethics for a wide variety of professions in 20 different countries and concluded that contemporary codes serve as (a) general statements of ethical principles that underpin the work of that profession, (b) declarations of ethical rules of general do's and don'ts, and (c) specific guidance relating to professional practice. For counselors and those they serve, the code of ethics serves a number of valuable purposes (see Table 1.2).

TABLE 1.2. USE AND PURPOSE OF CODES OF ETHICS

Our codes of ethics can
1. Guide professional behavior
2. Provide a strong prima facie reason for counselors to act in a certain way
3. Help protect our consumers
4. Pronounce to the public practice behaviors that are appropriate and those that are not
5. Facilitate a counselor's articulation of a professional identity
6. Profess our values and principles as a member of the counseling profession
7. Provide support, in cases of litigation, for practices that reflect the profession's standards
8. Enhance the status of counseling as a profession
9. Afford professional regulation of those in practice

Ethical Codes and Their Legal Connection

Similar to a code of ethics, laws provide guidelines as to what one may or may not do in a given situation. When viewed in relationship to our code of ethics, the law is generally supportive or neutral. The neutrality of the law is evident in that it typically allows the profession to "police" its members concerning adherence to the codes, intervening only when necessary to protect the welfare of the citizenry. However, laws can be supportive of professional standards. This is the case with laws that establish licensing requirements and function as a gatekeeper overseeing those who practice as a professional.

While codes of ethical behavior and law most often remain in their lanes, there are times when they exert influence over one another. Issues such as mandated reporting of child abuse and the duty to warn are significant legal mandates that have influenced our practice and have been reflected in our evolving codes of ethics. This may be best illustrated by the landmark decision in *Tarasoff v. Regents of the University of California* (1976). (See Case Illustration 1.2.)

CASE ILLUSTRATION 1.2

TARASOFF SUMMARY

The case involved Prosenjit Poddar, a University of California, Berkeley, graduate student; Tatiana Tarasoff, a woman he met at a dance class and with whom he became infatuated; and his therapist, Lawrence Moore, a psychologist at Berkeley's Cowell Memorial Hospital. Poddar presented as depressed and obsessed about Tarasoff and began stalking her. In his final session with Dr. Moore, he revealed that he intended to kill Tarasoff. Dr. Moore, having diagnosed him with an acute paranoid schizophrenic reaction, notified campus police and suggested he be placed in a psychiatric hospital for observation. After a brief detention, Poddar was released. He did not return to therapy and once again began to stalk Tarasoff. On October 27, 1959, he stabbed her to death.

In this case, while informing campus police about the risk factor Poddar presented, Dr. Moore did not inform Tarasoff or her family. Tarasoff's parents sued Dr. Moore and the university. While this case was initially dismissed on the grounds the doctor met his duty to warn, an appeal at the California Supreme Court level in 1974 found that mental health professionals do have a duty to warn clearly identified potential victims.

FOR REFLECTION AND DISCUSSION

1. In ruling on this case, the California Supreme Court found that mental health professionals do have a duty to warn clearly identified potential victims. What do criteria do you feel are necessary for defining "clearly identified potential victims"?
2. What if the client expresses a desire to do harm to "all of those lower-class people spending our tax money at the liquor store"? Is there a need to "warn" and, if so, whom and how?

The *Tarasoff v. Regents of the University of California* decision impacted the duties of mental health practitioners, especially concerning articulating the limits of confidentiality as part of gaining informed consent. Counselors now explain to clients that they will notify the authorities if the client is expressing the desire to harm others. In addition, counselors will explain that they have a duty to warn potential victims of actions that may be taken against them.

While the law has impacted the development of our code, our code has also served as a foundation for legal decisions. For example, in the case of *Ward v. Wilbanks* (2011), the Alliance Defense Fund brought suit on behalf of a former graduate student, Julea Ward, against the counselor education program at Eastern Michigan University. The suit was in response to the university's dismissal of Ward as a result of her refusal to counsel an individual on the basis of the client's sexual orientation. In ruling in favor of the university, Judge George Steeh of the Eastern District Court of Michigan affirmed the constitutional right for the counseling profession to designate protected classes such as race, ethnicity, gender, disability, age, and sexual orientation through the nondiscrimination section of the ACA Code of Ethics (ACA, 2005) and used this principle and its violation as the basis for the decision.

Keystones

- The establishment of a code of ethics signifies the maturation of a profession and results from the evolution of a collective professional identity within the organization.

- A code of ethics, regardless of the profession, provides a structure for the articulation of norms and expectations for practitioners.
- Professional codes of ethics are responsive to the changing societal mores as well as the expanding and changing demands placed on the professional.
- Our code of ethics reflects the values and moral principles collectively owned and espoused by the members of our profession.
- Our code calls us to (a) embrace the inherent worth and dignity of each client; (b) respect each client's uniqueness, autonomy, and right to self-determination; (c) honor human growth and development; and (d) respect the diversity within our clientele.
- Our code of ethics serves as a guide, a scaffold, for ethical and effective practice.
- The law is generally supportive or neutral, with both the code and the law mutually impacting each other.

Additional Resources

Print-Based

Ahia, C. E. (2009). *Legal and ethical dictionary for mental health professionals* (2nd ed.). University Press of America.

Consoli, A. J., Kim, B. S. K., & Meyer, D. M. (2008). Counselor's values profile: Implications for counseling ethnic minority clients. *Counseling and Values, 52,* 181–197.

Parsons, R. D., & Dickinson, K. L. (2017). *Ethical practice in the human services.* SAGE Publications.

Sisti, D. A., Caplan, A. L., & Rimon-Greenspan, H. (2014). *Applied ethics in mental health care: An interdisciplinary reader.* MIT Press.

Web-Based

Dobrin, A. (2012). Why ethics is hard. https://www.psychologytoday.com/us/blog/am-i-right/201202/why-ethics-is-hard

Josephson Institute of Ethics. http://josephsoninstitute.org/med-1makingsense/

Markkula Center for Applied Ethics. https://www.scu.edu/ethics/ethics-resources/ethical-decision-making/

References

American Counseling Association. (2005). *ACA code of ethics.*

American Counseling Association. (2014). *ACA code of ethics.*

American Psychological Association. (1953). *Ethical standards of psychologists.*

Banks, S. (2001). *Ethics and values in social work* (2nd ed.). Palgrave.

Bentham, J. (1948). *An introduction to the principles of morals and legislation.* Hafner Press. (Original work published 1780)

DeMitchell, T. A., Hebert, D. J., & Phan, L. T. (2013). The university curriculum and the Constitution: Personal beliefs and professional ethics in graduate school counseling programs. *Journal of College and University Law, 39,* 303–345.

Gorman, E. H., & Sandefur, 'Golden Age', quiescence, and revival: How the sociology of profession became the study of knowledge-based work. *Work and Occupations, 38,* 275–302.

Haas, L. J., & Malouf, J. L. (1995). *Keeping up the good work: A practitioner's guide to mental health ethics.*

Mabe, A., & Rollin, S. (1986). The role of a code of ethical standards in counseling. *Journal of Counseling and Development, 64,* 294–297.

Neukrug, E. (2000). *Theory, practice, and trends in human services: An introduction to an emerging profession* (2nd ed.). Belmont, CA: Wadsworth/Thomson Learning.

Pettifor, J. L. (2001). Are professional codes of ethics relevant for multicultural counseling? *Canadian Journal of Counseling, 35*(1), 26–35.

Riddick, F. (2003). The code of medical ethics of the American Medical Association. *Ochsner Journal, 5(2),* 6–10.

Sinclair, C., Simon, N., & Pettifor, J. (1996). The history of ethical codes and licensure. In L. Bass, S. DeMers. J. Ogloff, C. Peterson, J. Pettifor, R. Reaves, T. Retfalvi, N. Simon, C. Sinclair, & R. Tipton (Eds.), *Professional conduct and discipline in psychology* (pp. 1–15). American Psychological Association.

Tarasoff v. Regents of the University of California, 551 P.2d 334 (Cal.Sup.Ct., 1976).

Ward v. Wilbanks, No. 10-2100 (6th Cir., 2011).

Welfel, E. R., (2010*). Ethics in Counseling & Psychotherapy.* Boston, MA, Cengage.

Chapter 2

Ethics in Counseling
Navigating the Gray

… how to not get in trouble.

THE QUOTE ABOVE is perhaps the most common response when new counselors-in-training are asked what they hope to learn in their counseling ethics course work. The answer to that conundrum is as simple as it is unsatisfying to those who hear it: "It depends." Counseling ethics can be many things; a list of rules, a set of professional aspirations, the manifestation of our professional conscience. Ethics, however, are rarely if ever clear-cut. Regardless, counselors are expected to use the ethics of the profession as the basis for how they determine which course of action best serves their clients (ACA, 2014). The question then becomes, how are counselors expected to live up to that black-and-white expectation while navigating the "gray" that permeates counseling ethics?

The current chapter discusses the nature of and need for professional boundaries, as well as the unique challenges to the establishment and maintenance of boundaries in counseling in the digital age. After completing this chapter, readers will be able to

1. explain the principles that underpin ethical standards in counseling,
2. describe the ways personal morality intersects with professional ethics,
3. describe the structure and application of ethical codes in counseling practice, and
4. analyze specific factors that have an impact on ethics and practice in the field.

Ethics: A Guide Versus a Definitive Mandate

Ethics exist and are conceptualized differently across cultures, professions, institutions, and beyond. As a result, the way "ethics" in general is defined can vary slightly based on the context. Ahia (2009) defined ethics as a branch of study in philosophy concerning how people ought to act toward each other, pronouncing judgments of value about those actions. A hierarchy of values that permits choices to be made based on distinguished levels of right and wrong. (p. 27)

This definition helps illustrate the nature of ethics across contexts. What it does not do is describe ethics as a gateway to what many students and practitioners find themselves in search of: *a definitive mandate.*

Ethics is a philosophy born out of varying interpretations of right and wrong. As a result, ethical codes will always fall short of providing definitive steps for how to interpret every ethical dilemma a professional may face. In order to develop a framework for ethical decision making in the absence of definitive "rules," it helps to unpack some of the better-known theories associated with ethics. Keep in mind that these theories are not counseling specific. The degree to which a person subscribes to any of these theories, however, will have a major impact on the way in which they navigate counseling-specific ethics, a point that will be developed throughout this chapter.

As you review the following theories, you may discover that your own day-to-day decisions, both large and small, have been guided by many of the elements described in these theories. Exercise 2.1 is provided to help make ethics and the ethical theories described come alive in your own decision-making processes.

EXERCISE 2.1

REFLECTING ON PERSONAL DECISIONS

Directions: As you review the case illustration, consider each of the following questions.
1. How would you address the described issue?
2. What makes your decision "right" in that context?
3. Why is the basis for what is "right" and what is "wrong" different from one scenario to the next?
4. If a person can change their standards for right and wrong based on context, does right and wrong even exist in an objective sense?

Absolutism Versus Relativism

As the term implies, "absolutism" is the position that "right" and "wrong" are fixed. Put another way, it is the belief that there are things that are *always* right or *always* wrong, regardless of the context. Thus, the process of moral decision making is simply a matter of adopting a course of action that best adheres to what is right, regardless of the circumstances. For example, most have heard at some point that the act of stealing is "wrong." A broad analysis across various religious, cultural, political, and community ideologies would likely reveal that theft is largely considered immoral. Thus, from an ethical absolutism perspective, any course of action that involves theft is clearly "wrong," regardless of motivation, method, or outcome. A simple but equally absolute posture would be reflected by a counselor who believes that any physical contact with one's client is always an unethical boundary violation, regardless of the unique characteristics of the client or the nature and purpose of the contact.

Those embracing such an absolute perspective will find that the advantage of this perspective is that it provides definitive positions on right and wrong that a person can anchor themselves to when making decisions. The question is, can right and wrong truly remain a constant regardless of the context of the situation?

In contrast to absolutism, ethical relativism rejects the concept of universally applicable standards of right and wrong. Relativism is based on the idea that right and wrong is grounded in culture. Thus, what determines whether a decision is moral is whether it is considered acceptable within the culture that sets the backdrop for the decision-making process. Considering the incredible breadth of "culture" and how many different forms it can take, an advantage to relativism is clearly the flexibility in its application as one navigates a rarely black-and-white world. However, that same advantage can be considered a drawback in that the extent to which one's subjectivity can impact decision making creates a process that is riddled with the potential for personal and cultural biases to have an impact on the outcome. The challenge of such a relativistic perspective when employed in professional decision making is evident in the anxiety expressed by the counselor presented in Case Illustration 2.1.

CASE ILLUSTRATION 2.1

TELL ME WHAT TO DO!

Help, I'm panicking.

I am at my internship and am currently working with a young Asian woman. I feel like we have developed a very strong working alliance and have made some real progress in her career planning. Yesterday she brought me a gift as a thank-you. It is a little piece of pottery, and I don't think it is expensive, but it clearly has some real personal meaning and value to her.

I didn't know what to do. I know, or at least I think I knew, that we shouldn't take gifts because of professional boundaries, but she really wanted me to have it. So I took it.

Now I am wondering if that was unethical. So I asked my supervisor a simple question: "Should I keep it or thank her and return it next session?" I mean really, this concerns me.

The response she gave me was: "I don't know. Why does she want you to have it? What does she want in return? How does this fit into her family history, culture, and tradition?" Damn! I don't need more questions; I need her to "tell me what to do!"

Exercise 2.2 invites you to consider your own perspective—be it absolute, relative, or a combination of the two.

EXERCISE 2.2

PERSONAL PERSPECTIVE: ABSOLUTE OR RELATIVE

Directions: You may find that reviewing and discussing your response to each of the following will be aided by a discussion with a colleague, classmate, or supervisor.

1. Consider a recent experience with making a decision that you felt involved some level of "right" and "wrong" (i.e., moral characteristic).
    a. Which of the above ethical philosophies (i.e., absolutism vs. relativism) most closely guided your decision-making process?
    b. Had you used the other philosophy, would your decision have been different?
2. Can you identify an issue or decision (professional and personal) that is right or wrong "absolutely"?
3. Can you identify an issue or decision (professional and personal) that is only ever right or wrong "relative" to the context?

Utilitarianism Versus Deontology

Another set of common ethical philosophies often used when making decisions is utilitarianism and deontology. Utilitarianism is a philosophy in which right and wrong is grounded in and determined by the consequences of the decision being made. That is to say that in utilitarianism, the "right" decision is the one that does the most good for the greatest number of people. Morality is determined by outcomes, not absolutes. For example, if a hungry family of five is trying to decide where to have dinner, the "right" decision would be whichever restaurant is preferred by the majority. An advantage to this school of thought is that it takes the stakeholders (e.g., family members, clients, etc.) and their best interest into consideration. A disadvantage is that it fails to take into account the morality of the decision itself. Thus, an act or decision that is generally considered to be morally reprehensible could technically be considered "right" as long as it serves the most people. The ends justify the means.

Unlike utilitarianism, deontology does not concern itself with the consequences or outcomes of decisions. In deontology, similarly to absolutism, there are specific concepts, acts, and behaviors that are considered "right" regardless of context. Therefore, the consequences of a decision are less important than the morality of the decision itself. So, using the example above, consider the same family of five as they try to decide where to have dinner. Instead of trying to appease the majority, the parents in that scenario may decide that what is "right" (i.e., fair) is for everyone to have an opportunity to decide for the group. In that scenario, the right decision would be to allow whoever has yet to do so make the decision for the group. It is possible that whatever they select will disappoint the majority of the family. As mentioned above however, consequences are irrelevant in deontology. Therefore, if fairness is always moral, the decision would be the right one. Exercise 2.3 invites you to reflect on these two perspectives.

EXERCISE 2.3

PERSONAL PERSPECTIVE: UTILITARIANISM OR DEONTOLOGY

Directions: The following activity is best accomplished with a classmate, colleague, or supervisor.
1. Consider a recent experience with making a decision that you felt involved some level of "right" and "wrong" (i.e., moral characteristic).
   a. Which of the above ethical philosophies (i.e., absolutism vs. relativism) most closely guided your decision-making process?
   b. Had you used the other philosophy, would your decision have been different?
2. Identify a personal/professional role in which utilitarianism should dictate decision making. Why?
3. Identify a personal/professional role in which deontology should dictate decision making. Why?
4. Which of these schools of thought do you most often use to guide your decisions?

Principle Ethics

Earlier, you were exposed to ethical schools of thought commonly used to understand and guide the decision-making process. These philosophies are common, and individuals can see shades of them in nearly every corner of their lives where decisions are made. The question then is, what schools of thought dictate decision making in counseling? As with nearly all things ethical, there is no clear-cut answer. As a result, counselors are often left to reflect on their principles to guide them. Those principles were outlined in Chapter 1 and represent a more concrete set of agreed-upon values that are always considered in ethical decision making and from which counselors can inform their decisions (Meara et al., 1996). However, those principles are also flawed in that they may at times conflict. For example, a counselor may seek to protect a suicidal client (i.e., beneficence and nonmaleficence) by having them involuntarily committed against their wishes, thus failing to honor the client's autonomy.

Ethical Codes

As will be addressed in the next chapter, the decision-making process, ethical and otherwise, is multifaceted. That process is grounded in and dictated by the values of the decision maker. However, when it comes to making professional decisions, counselors are called on to "compartmentalize" their personal values and rely on the standards of the profession to guide them. Those standards are our ethical codes. Counseling ethics were born out of the philosophies addressed previously and are still simply a set of values dictated by a subjective interpretation of right and wrong. The source of that subjective interpretation is typically a collective; in the case of counseling, that collective includes organizations such the ACA and the American School Counseling Association. These codes have evolved over time to meet the needs of counselors and clients alike. Counseling ethics are ever evolving, thereby allowing the profession to be attentive to changes in the clients and communities we serve. Yet with that flexibility comes a system that can vary in specificity and purpose from one code to the next. Thus, it is important to have a sense of what counseling ethical codes are—and just as importantly, are not—in order to use them effectively.

The Purpose of Ethical Codes

The purpose and utility of ethical codes can differ from one code to the other. Broadly speaking, the bulk of counseling ethical codes serve to protect the well-being of clients in one way, shape, or form. Others are designed to protect counselors themselves. Regardless, the codes are typically inspired by one or more of the principles described previously. Where one can first see the codes begin to differ is in structure.

The Structure of Ethical Codes

As ethical codes evolve, there are often amendments or additions made in response to significant issues of the day. This has certainly been the case when considering the impact of technology on counseling (e.g., distance counseling).

The landscape of the field is ever changing, and as a result, it is impossible to develop an ethical code that can definitively guide a counselor through every dilemma they may face. Thus, the structure of each code can vary in terms of depth and specificity. While some may describe concrete directions, others provide general information on how to address a broader range of ethical concerns (Boccone, 2016). These are often referred to as mandatory and discretionary ethics.

Mandatory Ethical Codes

As the name suggests, mandatory ethical codes compel counselors to comply with specific outlined behaviors. These codes tend to be the most concrete and thus the easiest to comply with. They are particularly attractive to students or counselors consumed with the question of "how to not get in trouble." As Pope and Vasquez (2007) warned however, calibrating our ethical compass with only mandatory codes makes us vulnerable to missteps when dealing with the inevitable gray scenarios that all counselors face. That being said, mandatory codes typically take the form of either (a) obligatory or compulsory codes or (b) prohibitive or restrictive codes.

Obligatory codes describe ways in which counselors must act when faced with various ethical conundrums. For example, according to the ethical standards put forth by the ACA (2016), counselors are obligated to report to their superiors any agency practices or policies that could be considered inappropriate. In this code, the action counselors are mandated to take is relatively straightforward, and we can also see shades of the nonmaleficence principle that underline it.

Perhaps one of the best known and yet still highly debated obligatory code for counselors is related to their duty to warn. It is almost a certainty that at some point in every counselor's career, a client will reveal that they are a danger to themselves or others. In such cases, counselors are obligated to act, specifically by reporting the threat to the appropriate parties and doing everything in their power to ensure the safety of those involved. Although on the surface this code appears relatively straightforward, it should be noted that many debates continue in terms of what constitutes a danger significant enough to activate the counselor's obligation to warn. Recent questions have even been raised in terms of who the counselor is obligated to protect. For example, some have argued that the rise in animal-assisted therapy peripherally suggests the need of the profession to include animals (e.g., client pets) in the list of those we are mandated to protect (Gregorino, 2017).

Moving on from obligatory codes, prohibitive or restrictive codes describe actions that counselors are prohibited from engaging in. The best example of such a prohibition is likely found in Standard A.5.a of the ACA Code of Ethics (2016). This standard prohibits romantic relationships between counselors and their current client or the client's family members. There are a number of lesser known prohibited behaviors that are still important for the counselor to be aware of. For example, counselors are prohibited from any sort of forensic assessment for current or former clients. Take, for example, a counselor providing services to a romantic couple who were experiencing marital difficulty and considering divorce. Were that couple to ultimately decide to move forward with a divorce and then initiate legal proceedings to determine custody of their child, it would be unethical for their counselor to testify as to the appropriateness of each parent. Considering the previous relationship and the presumed insight the counselor already has into each party, this prohibition may seem counterintuitive (Boccone, 2016). Regardless, such an evaluation is expressly prohibited.

Discretionary Ethical Codes

Stude and McKelvey (1979) stated that ethical codes are meant to be interpreted based on the context of the issue in question. Corey et al. (2011) have suggested that we can best serve our clients when we actively monitor our own behaviors and challenge our thinking as it relates to the challenges we face. These practices seem particularly significant when it comes to navigating discretionary ethical codes. Although mandatory codes may be the preference of new professionals, the fact remains that there are an infinite number of ethical scenarios a counselor may face in a given day. Plainly put, no ethical code will ever be able to address them all.

This was illustrated in the example that pointed out that, although counselors are mandated to warn when working with a dangerous client, what constitutes a "dangerous client" is not set in stone and thus is ultimately determined by the individual counselor.

Unlike mandatory codes that dictate specific actions, discretionary codes provide counselors with considerations so that the decision-making process can be an informed one, grounded in the values of the profession (or the specific organization within that profession). One such example would be the ACAs (2016) ethical code related to bartering (Standard A.10.e). This code allows for the idea that bartering with clients in exchange for counseling could be either ethical or unethical, depending on the specific context and situation. Thus, this code dictates that counselors weigh each scenario individually and use their discretion to determine whether bartering is appropriate.

Multiple Ethical Codes

Professional identity is a major aspect of counselor development. As counselors-in-training advance in their training, they begin to find themselves aligned in various ways throughout the web of the helping professions. This may be dictated by their treatment modality of preference, the population they seek to serve, or the specific kinds of services they wish to provide. In all of those scenarios, one's professional identity development will likely lead to credentialing, as well as becoming a part of one or more professional organizations. What can easily be overlooked is that each of these credentialing bodies and professional organizations often comes with its own set of ethical codes, and counselors will be required to adhere to them all. It is easy to assume that these codes would be similar—and they often can be, particularly in major issues. Yet these codes are never identical, and differences certainly exist. Take, for example, the aforementioned ethical code that prohibits sexual relationships with clients. Such a relationship is strictly prohibited by most if not all mental health professions. If you consider sexual relationships with *past* clients, however, you start to see a distinction. The ACA, for example, will allow for a counselor to ethically engage in a romantic relationship with an ex-client as long as the interaction occurs at least 5 years after sessions are terminated. The APA (2017) has a similar standard but requires only a 2-year hiatus after termination.

Perhaps a simple straightforward set of rules to follow would be desirable. However, the human condition is neither simple nor straightforward. Additionally, the complex process of counseling cannot be reduced to formula and prescription. Therefore, variations in professional guidelines will continue to exist. In navigating such a multiplicity of ethical codes, a counselor may find some assistance with the embracing of a professional identity. It is the profession with which one identifies that will dictate the ethical standards they are compelled to uphold. Inevitably, counselors will face complex ethical issues, and their ability to determine the appropriate course of action will be dictated by their knowledge of the standards that are meant to guide them.

Keystones

- Ethics is a complex philosophical study of values that dictate right and wrong.
- No philosophical school of ethical thought stands above any other, and thus ethics remains a point of contention and debate.
- Ethics in counseling are grounded in professional principles and guide, rather than dictate, the behavior of counselor professionals.
- Ethical codes may be obligatory or discretionary; however, the interpretation of the counselor is always required, and the context of the issue is always significant.

Additional Resources

Print-Based

Cohen, E. D., & Cohen, G. S. (1999). *The virtuous therapist: Ethical practice of counseling and psychotherapy.* Brooks/Cole.

Keith-Spiegel, P. (2014). *Red flags in psychotherapy: Stories of ethics complaints and resolutions.* Routledge.

Web-Based

Birrell, P. J. (2006). An ethic of possibility: Relationship, risk, and presence. *Ethics & Behavior, 16,* 95–115.

Herlihy, B., & Dufrene, R. L. (2011). Current and emerging ethical issues in counseling: A Delphi study of expert opinions. *Counseling and Values, 56,* 10–24.

Herlihy, B., & Remley, T. P. (1995). Unified ethical standards: A challenge for professionalism. *Journal of Counseling and Development, 74,* 130–133.

Jordan, A. E., & Meara, N. M. (1990). Ethics and the professional practice of psychologists: The role of virtues and principles. *Professional Psychology: Research and Practice, 21,* 107–114.

Mabe, A. R., & Rollin, S. A. (1986). The role of a code of ethical standards in counseling. *Journal of Counseling and Development, 64,* 294–297.

Mannheim, C. I., Sancilio, M., Phipps-Yonas, S., Brunnquell, D., Somers, P., Farseth, G., & Ninonuevo, F. (2002). Ethical ambiguities in the practice of child clinical psychology. *Professional Psychology: Research and Practice, 33,* 24–29.

Zibert, J., Engels, D. W., Kern, C. W., & Durodoye, B. A. (1998). Ethical knowledge of counselors. *Counseling and Values, 43,* 34–48.

References

Ahia, C. E. (2009). *Legal and Ethical Dictionary for Mental Health Professionals.* University Press of American, Inc.

American Counseling Association. (2014). *ACA code of ethics.*

American Counseling Association. (2016). *ACA code of ethics.*

American Psychological Association. (2017). *Ethical principles of psychologists and code of conduct.*

Boccone, P. J. (2016). Ethical codes. In *SAGE encyclopedia of marriage, family, and couples counseling* (Vol. 4, pp. 563–565). SAGE Publications.

Corey, G., Corey, M., & Callanan, P. (2011). *Issues and ethics in the helping professions* (9th ed.). Brooks/Cole.

Gregorino, T. (2017, April). The case for including animals in counselors' duty to report. *Counseling Today.* http://www.ct.counseling.org

Meara, N. M., Schmidt, L. D., & Day, J. D. (1996). Principles and virtues: A foundation for ethical decisions, policies, and character. *Counseling Psychologist, 24,* 4–77.

Pope, K. S., & Vasquez, M. J. T. (2007). *Ethics in psychotherapy and counseling: A practical guide* (3rd ed.). Jossey-Bass.

Stude, E. W., & McKelvey, J. (1979). Ethics and the law: Friend or foe? *Personnel and Guidance Journal, 57,* 453–456.

Chapter 3

Models to Guide Ethical Decision Making

Counselors "are expected to engage in a carefully considered ethical decision-making process."

THE "WHAT" IS clear. Counselors are expected to engage in ethical decision making, a process involving "rational analysis geared toward identifying a resolution of an ethical dilemma" (Betan, 1997, p. 349). While this "what" is clear, the "how" of achieving this directive is not as clear.

In its statement of purpose, the ACA Code of Ethics states that counselors are expected to use a credible decision-making approach to resolving dilemmas: "When counselors are faced with ethical dilemmas that are difficult to resolve, they are expected to engage in a carefully considered ethical decision-making process" (ACA, 2014).

While directing its members to engage in ethical decision making, the ACA recognizes that there is no one decision-making model that is most effective in all situations. The directive, found within the Preamble of the American Counseling Code of Ethics, is for counselors to know and employ "*a model that can bear public scrutiny of its application*" [emphasis added] (ACA, 2014, p. 3).

A counselor has a large selection of models from which to choose. According to Cottone and Clause (2000), there are over 30 ethical decision-making models available. It is beyond the scope of this chapter to review all of the existing models. A brief review of several of these models reveals elements common to all; elements that when integrated can provide a useful template for guiding a counselor in ethical decision making. After completing this chapter, readers will be able to

1. describe what is meant by a practice-based model;
2. explain what is added to a counselor's decision-making process with the inclusion of an analysis of contextual variables, competing personal values, and involvement of stakeholders;
3. describe what is meant by a transcultural model of ethical decision making; and
4. identify the steps to ethical decision making.

Practice-Based Models

Practice-based models of ethical decision making have been derived from the experience of counselors in the field. A number of individuals have developed practice-based models for ethical decision making. The elements of two specific models, one created by Koocher and Keith-Spiegel (1998) and a second developed by Corey et al. (2014), are presented in Table 3.1. While each model is somewhat distinctive, there is more commonality than uniqueness in the steps described. These models, as is true for all practice-based models, are pragmatic and less theory specific or philosophically based. The models attempt to provide clear, practical guidelines for ethical decision making.

TABLE 3.1. **EXAMPLE OF PRACTICE-BASED MODELS**

Koocher & Keith-Spiegel, 1998		Corey et al., 2014	
Step	Description	Step	Description
1. Determine whether the matter truly involves ethics.	Discern whether the issue is more than just poor judgment or unorthodox or is a professional ethical issue.	1. Identify the problem or dilemma.	Recognize that there is a problem or dilemma. Determine the nature of the problem and gather the necessary information. Consult with the client frequently throughout the process.
2. Discover all the available facts before proceeding.	Resist the tendency to jump to conclusions or attribute meaning without gathering complete and accurate information. When the situation warrants it, gather information from all involved.	2. Identify the potential issues involved.	List and describe the relevant issues. List and assess the rights, responsibilities, and welfare of all those who are impacted by the situation, including family and friends. Consider the broader cultural issues that may impact the situation (e.g., race, socioeconomic status, etc.). Apply and prioritize the six moral principles to the situation, and identify where they might complement or come into conflict with one another.

CHAPTER 3 Models to Guide Ethical Decision Making   27

Koocher & Keith-Spiegel, 1998		Corey et al., 2014	
Step	Description	Step	Description
3. Consult existing guidelines that might apply.	Professional codes of ethics; policy statements; federal, local, and state law; and even writings on ethics may prove helpful in resolving the dilemma.	3. Review relevant ethical guidelines.	Review the ethical codes that apply to the situation, paying close attention to the cultural issues present. Reflect on your values to see if or where they might come into conflict with their association's code of ethics.
		4. Know relevant laws and regulations.	Counselors know and apply the laws and regulations that govern their practice.
4. Pause to consider all factors that might influence the decision.	Take time to increase awareness of any biases, prejudices, or personal needs that may distort perception of the dilemma and affect judgment and decision.		
5. Consult with a trusted colleague.	Discuss the dilemma with a colleague who is not only knowledgeable but also committed to ethical practice and willing to confront your perspective.	5. Obtain consultation.	Review issues and process with an unbiased colleague who can look beyond the counselors' own subjective impressions.
6. Evaluate the rights, responsibilities, and vulnerabilities of all affected parties.	To avoid flawed decisions, the rights of stakeholders (including, when relevant, institutions, communities, and the general public) need to be considered.		(similar to Corey step 7)
7. Generate alternative decisions.	Without considering the feasibility of options, generate an array of optional paths. Often what may appear as a less-than-desirable option may on reflection and without immediately being ruled out prove to be the best choice.	6. Consider possible and probable courses of action.	Identify all possible courses of action and consider the ethical, legal, and clinical ramifications of each solution.

Koocher & Keith-Spiegel, 1998		Corey et al., 2014	
Step	Description	Step	Description
8. Enumerate the consequences of making each decision.	Identifying the costs and risks of each option along with benefits resulting from each decision will not only help guide one's choice but also provide a rationale for the decision and resulting action.	7. List the consequences of the probable courses of action.	Consider the consequences of each action as they might play out, not only with the client but with any other constituent who may be involved.
9. Make the decision.	Using the data and consultation, decide on how to proceed.	8. Decide on what appears to be the best course of action.	Review all the gathered information and choose a course of action. Document your process, decision, implementation, and outcome.
10. Implement the decision.	While not always easy or comfortable, the chosen decision is now implemented. This step may require the development of a set of specific actions and ways to address possible impediments.		(implied in Corey's step 8)

It is clear that the two models described in Table 3.1 show minor variations in the number and descriptions of steps to be taken in ethical decision making, the general process of moving from the identification of problem to the selection and implementation of a path to follow are very similar. The process and utility of this general approach can be seen in the following brief case illustration and application (Case Illustration 3.1).

CASE ILLUSTRATION 3.1

A CHALLENGE TO CONFIDENTIALITY

Dr. Zhang received a request to complete an insurance form for his client. The client included a fax number and requested that the form be sent directly to him. After completing the form and faxing it to the number provided, Dr. Zhang realized that the number was to the client's office. Unsure of the security of the fax machine and aware that the insurance forms provided diagnosis, dates, and types of service, Dr. Zhang became concerned that he may have violated the client's confidentiality.

Dr. Zhang attempted to contact the client at work only to discover a recorded messaged noting that he was at home due to illness. Dr. Zhang called the client at home to inform him about the fax, but the client's girlfriend answered the call. Unsure of what the girlfriend knew about the client's relationship with the counselor, he merely said that it was not important and that he would call back.

Dr. Zhang, being quite concerned over the possibility of having violated confidentiality by faxing the insurance form, struggled with calling the client again and leaving a message with the girlfriend.

The fact that the information provided was not meant nor appropriate for the general public, and without knowledge of the level of security and privacy offered by the fax machine, an ethical violation may have occurred. Using the client's girlfriend to convey the information that the form was sent may invite questions that would place the client in a potentially uncomfortable situation **(identify the potential problem)**.

Dr. Zhang was concerned about having faxed the information without the client's written permission to fax and without knowing if the fax machine was HIPAA compliant. He was also concerned that if he shared information with the client's girlfriend, he may be violating ethical principles regarding confidentiality of records and documentations (ACA, 2014; Standard B.6.b) and respecting the dignity and welfare of the client (ACA, 2014; Standard A.1.a). In the process of discussing the situation with his colleague, Dr. Zhang recalled that the client was a sole proprietor and the sole occupant of his office space. Further, Dr. Zhang recalled that on one occasion the client's girlfriend dropped him off for his appointment **(consider all factors that might influence the decision)**.

Dr. Zhang realized that he now had two options: to do nothing, given the security of the office space, or to call back **(generate a course of action)**. In reviewing the options, he felt that the least costly option would be to do nothing, in that even a minimal disclosure to the client's girlfriend might invite a conversation between the client and his girlfriend that may not be welcomed **(list consequences)**. Dr. Zhang decided to let things stand as they were and to reach out to the client the next morning to see if he had gone to work and retrieved the fax **(decision)**.

FOR REFLECTION AND DISCUSSION
1. Dr. Zhang saw only two options ... do you see any others?
2. What do you see as possible negative consequences to Dr. Zhang's action and decision?

Integrative Model

Whereas practiced-based models target practical steps to be taken in developing an ethical response to a clinical dilemma, the integrative model (Tarvydas, 1998) of resolving ethical dilemmas shines a light on the morals, beliefs, and experiences of those involved. Tarvydas (1998) described a four-stage integrative decision-making model that invites counselors to include an understanding of the context and engagement with all stakeholders in making decisions involving ethical dilemmas. The stages are described in Table 3.2.

TABLE 3.2. INTEGRATIVE MODEL

Stage I: Interpreting the situation through awareness and fact finding	The counselor needs to be aware of the unique challenges experienced within their field of specialization and be able to examine the situation as it may constitute an ethical dilemma. In situations in which a dilemma occurs, the counselor is also aware of the parties affected and their ethical stance in the situation.
Stage II: Formulating an ethical decision	Very similar to a practiced-based mode, this stage requires the counselor to review the problem correctly to determine what ethical codes, standards, principles, and institutional policies are pertinent to this type of situation. Once this has been accomplished, the counselor needs to generate a list of potential courses of action, along with the positive and negative consequences for following each one, and select the best course of action.
Stage III: Selecting an action by weighing competing nonmoral values	As part of the selection process, the counselor analyzes the course of action from the perspective of personal competing values and contextual values (e.g., institutional, team, collegial, and societal/cultural). This step helps ensure that possible bias, prejudice, or simply personal blind spots are resolved before making the final decision on the course of action.
Stage IV: Planning and executing course of action	The counselor determines the concrete actions that need to be taken, with consideration given to the potential obstacles to taking that course of action, including those reflecting contextual barriers.

The model's inclusion of the analysis of contextual variables, competing personal values, and involvement of stakeholders makes it compatible with elements of multicultural theory and practice. This model also uses virtue ethics and an emphasis on behavioral strategies, which is consistent with a multicultural approach as well. While compatible with multicultural approaches to counseling, it is limited in its analysis of cultural variables that might play a role in the process of ethical decision making.

The Transcultural Integrative Model

The transcultural integrative model of ethical decision making (Garcia et al., 2003) addresses the need for inclusion of multicultural theory into ethical decision making and emphasizes the engagement of specific counselor attitudes as central to ethical decision making. The model highlights the need for counselors to possess specific attitudes and characteristics, including those identified by Tarvydas (1998) and Welfel (2002). These include (a) reflection, (b) attention to context, (c) balance, (d) collaboration, and (e) tolerance. Table 3.3 provides a description of each of these attitudes.

TABLE 3.3. **COUNSELOR ATTITUDES ESSENTIAL TO MULTICULTURAL ETHICAL DECISION MAKING**

Reflection	Reflection concerns counselors' awareness of their feelings, values, and skills, as well as understanding those of the other stakeholders involved in the situation.
Context	Attention to context involves being attentive to the factors that may play a role in the situation; namely, the team, institutional policy, society, and culture.
Balance	Counselors maintain balance by weighing each of the issues and perspectives presented by all individuals involved.
Collaboration	Collaboration means that counselors must maintain the attitude of inviting all parties to participate in the decision to whatever extent possible.
Tolerance	Counselors display tolerance by being accepting of the diverse worldviews, perspectives, and philosophies of the different stakeholders.

While many of the steps and processes employed in a transcultural integrative approach to ethical decision making parallel those of a practice-based model, this approach highlights the need for increased sensitivity, awareness, and inclusion of multicultural elements in the process.

The first step in the transcultural approach is similar to most other decision-making models in that it directs counselors to gather data necessary for identifying the nature and expanse of the dilemma. The uniqueness of this model is that it highlights the need for counselors to understand how the dilemma may affect different stakeholders who may have a different or even opposing worldview. This step requires that counselors have an awareness of their own cultural identity and the degree to which this may affect their view of the dilemma. Case Illustration 3.1 provides a brief description of how a variance in worldview can impact what is seen as an ethical dilemma.

The second step of the transcultural integrative model of ethical decision making parallels that of practice-based models, with the addition of incorporating specific cultural elements into the formulation of the decision. With this as the operative model, counselors will (a) review all cultural information gathered in step 1, (b) review potential discriminatory laws or institutional regulations, (c) make sure that the potential courses of action reflect the different worldviews involved, (d) consider the positive and negative consequences of opposing courses of action from the perspective of the parties involved, (e) consult with cultural experts if necessary, and (f) select a course of action that best represents an agreement of the parties involved.

When applied to our case of Ms. Wilson and Maria in Case Illustration 3.1, the counselor may engage Maria in an interpersonal process of "consensualizing" the situation (Cottone, 2001). The goal would be for them to agree to the conditions of Maria's reality, including contextual influences, and the specific needs that she is attempting to satisfy. One outcome of such a process might be an agreement to include Maria's parents in the process of assessing the costs and benefits of Maria forgoing college for the family business or going to college and forgoing the immediate engagement in the business. The goal of such a discussion would be

CASE ILLUSTRATION 3.2

A POTENTIAL CONFLICT OF VALUES

Tanya Wilson, a high school counselor, finds herself in conflict regarding her ability to counsel and support a very bright Hispanic student. Maria is an honors student who excels in the areas of mathematics and science. Ms. Wilson, who highly values education and the need for women in the sciences, is excited to inform Maria that she has been awarded a full scholarship to the Massachusetts Institute of Technology. Maria expressed her gratitude for the affirmation and support that Ms. Wilson had provided. However, she told Ms. Wilson that she had decided not to go to college following graduation. She explained that she had decided to stay at home and help her parents with their small family-run restaurant. Maria's resistance to pursuing higher education concerned Ms. Wilson. She was aware that this "concern" was more than that which she had for all her students. She wondered whether her own strong valuing of education and her hope that Maria would truly be a trailblazer for other girls at the school were causing her strong emotional reaction. In reflection, she became aware that she was struggling to support Maria's autonomy in deciding to remain in the community rather than pursue the path that she (Ms. Wilson) felt was the best course of action. Ms. Wilson was concerned that her vision and values were interfering with her desire to respect Maria's values and autonomy.

FOR REFLECTION AND DISCUSSION

1. Assume that Ms. Wilson turns to you for consultation. What are the issues involved in this case, and how would you advise?
2. How might issues of informed consent, boundaries, and competence be playing out in this illustration?

to identify a path that had the highest potential for meeting all of Maria's needs, in light of her cultural values.

The third step engages the counselor and client in the process of weighing potentially competing, nonmoral values that may interfere with the execution of the course of action selected. For Maria, even if it is assumed that her parents would support her choice to go to college, it is possible that her learned gender role and enculturated value of the centrality of family might be challenging to her engagement in a path that results in her moving away from her home and family.

The final step in a transcultural model of ethical decision making directs the counselor to carry out the plan, document the actions taken, and carefully evaluate the consequences of the ethical decision. In a case such as Maria's, the counselor may wish to help Maria and her family prepare for the impact of such a significant change in their family history. The counselor would also do well to help Maria anticipate and prepare for potential biases, discrimination, stereotypes, and prejudices she may encounter as a Latina coming from a lower socioeconomic background and entering a prestigious university and a predominately White male field of study.

Counselor Value-Based Conflict Model

Legal actions (e.g., *Keeton v. Anderson-Wiley et al.*, 2010; *Walden v. Centers for Disease Control & Prevention*, 2012) have highlighted the need to strive for that which is in the best interest of our clients while at the same time acknowledging the conflicts that can arise when client behaviors, lifestyle, and even counseling goals differ from counselors' deeply held personal beliefs and values. In response to the realities of such value-based conflicts, Kocet and Herlihy (2014) developed the counselor values-based conflict model (CVCM).

It is clear that even when a client's behavior or counseling goals appear unacceptable to the counselor, the counselor's personal values do not negate the duty to provide competent services. In addressing such ethical dilemmas, CVCM invites counselors to employ a process of *ethical bracketing*.

The concept of ethical bracketing recognizes the reality that counselors are not—nor can they be—value-free and totally objective in their interactions with clients. In fact, such a stance would negate the value of authenticity and genuineness. Thus, we engage in ethical practice not by denying our values and beliefs but by recognizing them and ensuring that we do not impose them on our clients. Conflicts between what the counselor personally believes and values and what the client believes and values are inevitable. Ethical bracketing, as applied to ethical decision making, requires the counselor to intentionally separate personal values from professional values and to engage in steps that will allow the counselor to set aside these personal values in order to provide ethical and appropriate counseling (Kocet & Herlihy, 2014).

The steps involved in such ethical bracketing include the following:

- immersion in a self-reflective process about the nature of the values conflict
- education about the various codes of ethics and professional literature on best practices
- consultation and supervision with trusted colleagues who can provide ongoing feedback about the specific values conflict
- personal counseling to help manage and remediate any identified barriers and/or personal bias that prevent the counselor from forming
- when permitted by the client, engagement with another counselor as co-counselor in the therapeutic relationship

A Practical, Culturally Sensitive Model for Ethical Decision Making

While the previous discussion highlights the uniqueness of individual approaches to ethical decision making, it also reveals the core or common elements that run across these various models. Recurring elements have been categorized as

> ***Awareness*** of the existence and nature of the dilemma along with personal values and biases; ***Grounding*** in both knowledge of the professional codes of practice, laws and institutional policies and procedures; ***Support*** which is found via consultation with all

parties involved and professional colleagues and supervisors and finally; **Implementation** including documentation and evaluation. (Parsons & Dickinson, 2017, p. 169)

These elements—along with the specifics provided in the works of Holly Forester-Miller and Thomas Davis (2016), Ruth Ann Tavydas (2012), and Jorge Garcia et al. (2003)—have been merged to create a practical, culturally sensitive model for ethical decision making, which is presented below.

Step 1: Preparing for Ethical Practice

The first stage to ethical decision making occurs prior to engagement with an ethical dilemma. Counselors seeking to engage in ethical decision making must approach practice with a fundamental knowledge of the principles and values that are foundational to professional counseling. It is essential to understand the code of ethics currently applicable as well as the significant laws and statutes governing practice. Because ethical decision making is personal as well as professional, it is essential to gain clarity over one's worldview with its bias, prejudices, and situations in which self-interest will make it hard to make the right ethical choices. It is worth noting here that worldviews can and do evolve over time, as have the ethical mandates of the profession. Therefore, this pursuit for clarity is an ongoing endeavor that will continue throughout one's professional career.

Step 2: Identifying the Problem

When encountering a challenge or dilemma in one's practice, it is essential to take time to examine the situation to determine if an ethical dilemma exists. It is possible that what is being experienced is a clinical or professional issue, rather than one of ethics. It is also possible that the issue being confronted has legal implications. Thus, it is important to gather data that allows for a very concrete and specific articulation of the issues being addressed. During this step, it is also important to broaden the perspective to determine all of the stakeholders who may be affected by the situation. In this process, it is essential to be aware of the possibility of the unique impact on those with different or even opposing worldviews.

Step 3: Formulating the Ethical Concern

This step requires counselors to review the situation through the lenses of our professional code of ethics, the values and principles underlying those codes, and the particular institutional policies that may be applicable to the situation. Beyond consideration of the ACA Code of Ethics (ACA, 2014), practitioners need to understand the codes governing their particular specialty practice, as well as any state or unique professional codes applicable (Brennan, 2013). As with each step in our ethical decision making, special attention should be given to any multicultural issues that may be involved in a particular case (Frame & Williams, 2005).

Step 4: Determining of the Nature and Dimensions of the Dilemma

Before developing a plan of action or response to the dilemma being experienced, the problem and its potential impact need to be assessed. Consulting current professional literature as well as experienced professionals is a valuable tool for gaining an expanded perspective on the issues at hand. It is essential to examine not only the dilemma's implications for each of the foundational principles—autonomy, justice, beneficence, nonmaleficence, fidelity—but also the potential impact on all stakeholders and institutions involved, the community, and the general public.

Step 5: Generating Potential Courses of Action

It is useful to engage a colleague, supervisor, or professional consultant in a brainstorming process to generate a number of possible courses of action. As is true anytime a process of brainstorming is employed, judgment should be suspended when focusing on a goal of developing numerous, creative possibilities. Evaluation as to the quality of the various courses of action will come later. For now, the goal is to think broadly and creatively. It is important to monitor the possible effect that one's bias or prejudices may have in limiting options that may be created.

Step 6: Assessing Options

This step involves assessing each of the options generated regarding its potential costs and benefits. It is essential to consider the potential impact on all of the stakeholders involved. It is also important to consider personal and contextual barriers, as well as competing values, since they may affect the implementation of any of the paths developed.

When evaluating the options, it is important to consider each of the following:

1. Is the option "fair" to all parties involved?
2. If the ethical decision were to be known by family, friends, or colleagues or printed in the newspaper, would you be comfortable with the decision that had been made?
3. Does the option support professional values and principles, such as (a) do no harm, (b) promote client well-being and autonomy, and (c) protect the integrity of the profession?
4. Which option will result in the best consequences or results?
5. Which option is consistent with the most important ethical principles and avoids creating another ethical challenge?

Step 7: Selecting and Implementing a Course of Action

Given the outcome of the assessment phase, the counselor needs to select and implement the final decision. Going through the steps of the decision-making model will increase the possibility that the decision chosen is the best that could have been derived given the circumstances. This does not mean that the decision need be the ultimate, final decision made. If additional information comes to light and as a result changes the perspective on the decision made, the ethical counselor will revisit the issue, even when the decision cannot be rescinded or modified. Revisiting the steps taken will help strengthen one's ability to engage in such an ethical decision-making process should it be needed in the future.

Step 8: Documenting the Steps Taken

As is true for most of our practice decisions, it is valuable for a counselor to document the steps taken when attempting to address an ethical conflict. In the text, *Documentation in Counseling Records: An Overview of Ethical, Legal, and Clinical Issues,* Mitchell (2007) points out that the 21st-century counselor's reality includes increased lawsuits and allegations of unethical conduct. Given this backdrop and the expectations that such legal action will increase in the future, documentation—especially that demonstrating adherence to professional codes of conduct—is vital.

Table 3.4 provides a summary listing of the steps to be taken when engaging in ethical decision making. In addition, questions are provided as an aide to the application of the model to one's own practice experience.

TABLE 3.4. QUESTIONS—GUIDING ETHICAL DECISION MAKING

Predecision Preparation
- Am I knowledgeable of the latest code of ethics?
- Is the latest version of the code of ethics available?
- Am I familiar with some of the contemporary challenges to ethical practice?
- Am I aware of my values, prejudices, biases, and views of self and others?
- Am I aware of those areas of need or self-interest that may come under challenge in an ethical dilemma?

Identifying the Problem
- What are the facts of the situation?
- Is this a personal problem?
- Is this a clinical problem?
- Is this a legal problem?
- Is this an ethical problem?
- Is it more than one of the above?
- Is legal advice needed?
- How might the problem be viewed by one having a different worldview?

Formulating the Ethical Concern
- How might the dilemma relate to specific principles listed in the professional code of ethics?
- How might the dilemma relate to institutional policies of the context in which you experienced the dilemma?
- How might the dilemma relate to your own values?
- How might the dilemma relate to your worldview?
- Does the dilemma tap into your own personal needs, biases, or prejudices?

Determining the Nature and Dimensions of the Dilemma
- What implications might this have for the principle of autonomy?
- What implications might this have for the principle of nonmaleficence?
- What implications might this have for the principle of beneficence?
- What implications might this have for the principle of justice?
- What implications might this have for the principle of fidelity?
- What are the possible impacts of this dilemma on all stakeholders?

Generating Potential Courses of Action
- Have you brainstormed possible courses of action (being nonjudgmental as to feasibility)?
- Have you engaged a colleague in the process?

Assessing Options
- What is the possible impact (both positive and negative) of each course of action on the client (including physical, psychological, and social realms)?
- What is the possible impact on the principles of doing no harm and promoting the welfare of the client?
- What is the possible impact (both positive and negative) of each course of action on other stakeholders (family, friends, and coworkers)?
- What is the possible impact (both positive and negative) of each course of action on the client's community?
- What is the possible impact (both positive and negative) of each course of action on the public view of the counseling profession?
- How will the option look to others once it is known?
- Would this option be applied to others in similar circumstances?
- Would this option be recommended to a colleague in a similar situation?

Selecting and Implementing a Course of Action
- Are the needed resources available for the implementation of the selected course of action?
- Is there a set plan or steps in place to support implementation?

Documenting the Steps Taken
- Have I recorded not only the decisions I have made but the resources I employed in making those decisions?
- Does my documentation adequately convey my desire to tend to the welfare of my client while adhering to laws and regulations governing my practice?
- Is the confidentiality of my client maintained even in the process of documenting the issues and the dilemmas I encountered?

Throughout the upcoming chapters, we will focus on specific areas of ethical concern and employ this model in deriving our decision. Exercise 3.1 invites you to attempt applying the steps and questions that serve as the core of this model to a few potentially conflicting situations.

EXERCISE 3.1

EMPLOYING A DECISION-MAKING MODEL

Directions: Below you will find a brief description of three situations that could prove ethically challenging. It is suggested that you use the steps and questions found in Table 3.4 to arrive at an ethically sound decision. You may find it beneficial to engage in this exercise with a classmate or colleague.

Situation 1: You work as a high school counselor. You have been working with a student, a 19-year-old with Down syndrome, who attempts to hug you at the end of each session.

Situation 2: During a termination session, your client presents you with a handmade, vintage lithograph that she got from her home in China.

Situation 3: You are on vacation at a seaside resort. One evening at dinner you recognize a couple you have seen in couples counseling. They invite you to join them for a drink.

Keystones

- Counselors are expected to be familiar with a credible model of decision making that can bear public scrutiny and its application.
- A practice-based model is one that is derived from experience and intended to serve as a practical guide for counselors.
- Whereas practiced-based models target practical steps to be taken in developing an ethical response to a clinical dilemma, the integrative model (Tarvydas, 1998) shines a light on the morals, beliefs, and experiences of those involved.
- Tarvydas (1998) described a four-stage integrative decision-making model that requires professionals to use reflection, balance, attention to the context, and collaboration in making decisions involving ethical dilemmas.
- The transcultural integrative model of ethical decision making (Garcia et al., 2003) addresses the need for inclusion of multicultural theory in ethical decision making.
- Many of the steps and processes employed in a transcultural integrative approach to ethical decision making parallel those of a practice-based model. However, this approach emphasizes the need for increased sensitivity, awareness, and inclusion of multicultural elements in the process.

- A model incorporating elements of practice-based, integrative, and transcultural models of decision making starts with a counselor's predilemma understanding of the codes of ethics, laws, and regulations governing practice and institutional policies.
- Steps included in an expanded model for ethical decision making include (a) preparing for ethical practice, (b) identifying the problem, (c) formulating the ethical concern, (d) determining the nature and dimensions of the dilemma, (e) generating potential courses of action, (f) assessing options, and (g) selecting and implementing a course of action.

Additional Resources

Print-Based

British Association for Counselling and Psychotherapy (BACP). (2015). *Ethical framework for the counseling professions.*

Garcia, J. G., Froehlich, R. J., Cartwright, B., Letiecq, D., Forrester, L. E., & Mueller, R. O. (1999). Ethical dilemmas related to counseling clients living with HIV/AIDS. *Rehabilitation Counseling Bulletin, 43,* 41–50.

Herlihy, B., & Corey, G. (2014). *ACA ethical standards casebook* (7th ed). American Counseling Association.

Luke, M., Goodrich, K. M., Gilbride, D. D., (2013). Intercultural model of ethical decision making: Addressing worldview dilemmas in school counseling. *Counseling and Values 58*(2), 177–194.

Web-Based

Center for Ethical Practice. http://www.centerforethicalpractice.org/publications/models-mary-alice-fisher-phd/ethical-decision-making-model/

Forester-Miller, H., & Davis, T. E. (2016). Practitioner's guide to ethical decision making (Rev. ed.). http://www.counseling.org/docs/default-source/ethics/practioner's-guide-to-ethical-decision-making.pdf

Francis, P. C., & Dugger, S. M. (2014). Professionalism, ethics, and value-based conflicts in counseling: An introduction to the special section. *Journal of Counseling & Development, 92,* 131–134. http://dx.doi.org/10.1002/j.1556-6676.2014.00138.x

Markkula Center for Applied Ethics. (2014). The ethical decision making assistant: Making an ethical decision app (Version 1.0) [Mobile application software]. https://www.scu.edu/ethics-app//

Your CEUS. (2019). Your source for counseling CE. https://www.yourceus.com/

References

American Counseling Association. (2014). *ACA code of ethics.*

Betan, E. J. (1997). Toward a hermeneutic model of ethical decision making in clinical practice. *Ethics and Behavior, 7,* 347–365.

Brennan, C. (2013). Ensuring ethical practice: Guidelines for mental health counselors in private practice. *Journal of Mental Health Counseling, 35* (3), 245–261.

Corey, G., Corey, M. S., Corey, C., & Callanan, P. (2014). *Issues and ethics in the helping professions* (9th ed.). Brooks/Cole.

Cottone, R. R. (2001). A social constructivism model of ethical decision-making in counseling. *Journal of Counseling & Development, 79,* 39–45.

Cottone, R. R., & Claus, R. E. (2000). Ethical decision-making models: A review of the literature. *Journal of Counseling and Development, 78,* 275–283.

Forester-Miller, H., & Davis, T. (1996). *A practitioner's guide to ethical decision making.* American Counseling Association.

Forester-Miller, H., & Davis, T. E. (2016). Practitioner's guide to ethical decision making (Rev. ed.). http://www.counseling.org/docs/default-source/ethics/practioner's-guide-to-ethical-decision-making.pdf

Frame, M. W., & Williams, C. B. (2005). A model of ethical decision making from a multicultural perspective. *Counseling and Values, 49,* 165–179.

Garcia, J. G., Cartwright, B., Winston, S. M., & Borzuchowska, B. (2003). A transcultural integrative model for ethical decision making in counseling. *Journal of Counseling & Development 81(30),* 268–278.

Keeton v. Anderson-Wiley et al., No. 1:10-CV-00099-JHR-WLB, 733 F. Supp. 2d 1368 (S.D. Ga. 2010).

Kocet, M. M., & Herlihy, B. J. (2014). Addressing value-based conflicts within the counseling relationship: A decision-making model. *Journal of Counseling & Development, 92(2),* 180–186.

Koocher, G. P. & Keith-Spiegel, P. (1998). *Ethics in psychology: Professional standards and cases.* Oxford University Press.

Mitchell, R. W. (2007). *Documentation in counseling records: An overview of ethical, legal, and clinical issues* (3rd ed.). American Counseling Association.

Parsons, R. D., & Dickinson, K. L. (2017). *Ethical practice in the human services.* SAGE Publications.

Tarvydas, V. M. (2012). Ethics and ethical decision-making. In D. R. Maki & V. M. Tarvydas (Eds.), *The professional practice of rehabilitation counseling* (p. 339–370). New York, NY: Springer Publishing Company, LLC.

Tarvydas, V. M. (1998). Ethical decision-making processes. In R. R. Cottone & V. M. Tarvydas (Eds.), *Ethical and professional issues in counseling* (pp. 144–154). Prentice Hall.

Walden v. Centers for Disease Control & Prevention, No. 10-11733 (669 F.3d 1277 2012).

Welfel, E. R. (2002). *Ethics in counseling and psychotherapy: Standards, research, and emerging issues.* Brooks/Cole.

21st-Century Challenges to Ethical Practice

II

Chapter 4

Practice in a Diverse World

She has a Presidential scholarship and can be the first person in her family to go to college, but she told me she is going to stay home and work in her family's restaurant like her siblings have done.

THE COUNSELOR QUOTED in the opening of this chapter is sharing his confusion about the decision being made by one of his students. Valentina is an academically gifted, first-generation Mexican American student who has been accepted, with a full scholarship, to five first-tier universities. The counselor's confusion centers on her decision to forgo her expressed desire to become a geneticist and fulfill her family's expectations that she stay at home and work in the family restaurant, just as her sister and brother have done. The counselor's confusion appears to rest in his failure to understand and be sensitive to the principle of "familism," a multidimensional construct composed of core values that include strong family identification, attachment, mutual support, interconnectedness, responsiveness to family obligation, and the value of subjugating the self for family (Lugo Steidel & Contreras, 2003).

As counselors, we are committed to empowering our clients to accomplish their mental health, wellness, education, and career goals (Kaplan et al., 2013). However, it is essential that we embed this commitment within a sensitivity and respect for diverse values, mores, and traditions and how these color the definition of these goals.

Counselors in the 21st century need to become more competent with respect to issues of multiculturalism and diversity. Counselors need to increase their sensitivity and competency with clients of diverse racial and ethnic backgrounds as well as those of different ability status, sexual orientation, socioeconomic status, and spirituality.

This call for increased sensitivity and competency in working with a diverse population is not only a practical directive but also an ethical mandate. As noted in the ACA Code of Ethics, in the introduction to Section A: The Counseling Relationship, "Counselors actively attempt to understand the diverse cultural backgrounds of the clients they serve. Counselors also explore their own cultural identities and how these affect their values and beliefs about the counseling process" (ACA, 2014, p. 4).

The current chapter presents the challenges encountered by counselors of the 21st century as they respond to the needs of a diverse client population and the ethical mandates of their profession. After completing this chapter, readers will be able to

1. explain the importance of counselors increasing their awareness of their cultural values and biases;
2. describe the attitudes, knowledge, and skills necessary to increase a counselor's awareness of their client's worldview;
3. explain the ethical considerations guiding the selection of assessment approaches and intervention strategies when engaging with diverse client populations; and
4. describe the attitudes, knowledge, and skills required for the application of culturally appropriate interventions and helping strategies.

A Challenge to Our Professional Assumptions

Much of the theory and practice of mental health, including counseling, has emerged from Western cultural traditions and Western understandings of the human condition. As our profession has increased knowledge of and respect for the varying cultures, beliefs, and traditions of those whom we serve, we have found a number of our Western-based assumptions underlying counseling theory and practice challenged.

Research (e.g., Biswas et al., 2016; Nguyen & Bornheimer, 2014) highlights the fact that health and illness are perceived differently across cultures and that this cultural meaning impacts whether individuals seek treatment and what type of treatment may be sought (U.S. Department of Health and Human Services, 2001). Standards that we typically employ to define mental health and emotional well-being are now viewed as culturally relative. Many of the fundamental "truths" on which we as counselors have based our decisions—"truths" such as the definition of what is "normal," the universality of linear thinking, and our focus on the individual and psychological primacy of independence—are now being reconsidered in light of our understanding of cultural diversity (Sue & Sue, 1999). Our heightened awareness of the value and role of culture as a factor affecting the delivery of professional services has resulted in an evolution of our professional practice and the ethics guiding that practice.

Sensitivity to Diversity and Minority Experience

Culture is a significant factor in both the definition of what is problematic and the approach to a resolution that are acceptable to a diverse client population (Hernandez et al., 2009). Ethical counselors need to be sensitive to the influence of culture and the strains that can exist when clients operate from a worldview different from that of their counselors.

This challenge is compounded by the reality that many clients present with diverse and often oppressive experiences as a result of simultaneously belonging to multiple minority groups. For example, Black women by definition have identities in dual minorities (i.e., being Black and being women). This can be compounded by holding membership in a third minority group; for example, a Black lesbian woman.

The ethical counselor recognizes the ways clients are impacted by their multiple marginalized identities and by systems of oppression (e.g., racism, ethnocentrism, sexism, heterosexism, and nativism). The ethical counselor must be sensitive not simply to the singularity of culture but to the intersectionality of many different aspects of one's social identity and the impact of systems and processes of oppression and domination on clients (Hankivsky & Cormier, 2009). Further, while attending to the needs and goals of their clients, the ethical counselor who is sensitive to diverse experiences will be prepared to respond as an advocate for social justice in response to the experiences of their clients.

Diversity and the Counseling Relationship

One of the primary considerations for the counselor in the 21st century working with those holding a different worldview is to examine the possible impact that such diversity may have on the counseling relationship and dynamic. Lee & Diaz (2009) introduced the term "cross-cultural zone" to describe the nature of a helping relationship when the counselor differs significantly from the client in terms of cultural background. While it may be argued that it is ideal for counselor and client to share a similar culture (Marsella, 2011), the reality, given the increasing diversity of our client base, reduces the possibility of such concordance of worldview.

Working within the cross-cultural zone requires a counselor to embrace a broader perspective on culture and recognize that Western-based psychological theory may not directly translate to an application with other cultures. The ethical counselor is aware, for example, that traditional ways of interpreting body language and eye contact may be inaccurate—and even the practice of engaging in open-ended questions may be misinterpreted—if not viewed with a culturally sensitive lens. Some clients—for example, Native Americans and Asian Americans—may view typical Western communication patterns as invasive. Recognizing and being sensitive to cultural differences is essential for establishing the trust necessary for the establishment of a working alliance and is highlighted as an ethical principle guiding professional practice.

> Counselors communicate information in ways that are both developmentally and culturally appropriate. Counselors use clear and understandable language when discussing issues related to informed consent. When clients have difficulty understanding the language that counselors use, counselors provide necessary services (e.g., arranging for a qualified interpreter or translator) to ensure comprehension by clients. In collaboration with clients, counselors consider the cultural implications of informed consent procedures and, where possible, counselors adjust their practices accordingly. (ACA, 2014, Principle A.2.c, p.4)

Another component of the professional relationship that calls for a counselor's increased sensitivity to cultural meaning is in the area of confidentiality and privacy. Cultures that are more collectivist in orientation approach the issue of confidentiality differently than do cultures that emphasize individualism (Glosoff & Kocet, 2006). Case Illustration 4.1 highlights this challenge.

CASE ILLUSTRATION 4.1

A VIOLATION OF PRIVACY?

The following is a brief reflection from Tammy Bringaze, a member of the Ethics Revision Task Force, reported in Kaplan et al. (2009):

> I work with Afghan refugees, and the idea of confidentiality has a very different meaning in their culture. It is much more communal. There is really the sense among the Afghans of trying to look out for one another and pull together. The other day, I had an Afghan woman come in and sit down in the middle of another woman's session, and neither blinked an eye. (p. 247)

FOR REFLECTION AND DISCUSSION

1. Given the potential legal considerations surrounding confidentiality, how would you address the scenario described?
2. In addition to issues of confidentiality, what other concerns (ethical and/or practical) might you have if placed in a similar situation?

Clearly, for a counselor who was not sensitive to the Afghan culture, the presence of this "other" may be viewed as an intrusion and a violation of the confidential nature of the counseling relationship. Without such awareness and cultural sensitivity, a counselor might undermine the therapeutic alliance by asking the person to leave, something that could be seen as a violation of the client's cultural values. The importance of counselors being aware of and sensitive to the cultural meanings of privacy and confidentiality is specified in the ACA Code of Ethics: "Counselors maintain awareness and sensitivity regarding cultural meanings of confidentiality and privacy. Counselors respect differing views toward disclosure of information. Counselors hold ongoing discussions with clients as to how, when, and with whom information is to be shared" (ACA, 2014, Principle B.1.a, p. 6).

Assessment, Diagnosis, and Problem Identification

When viewing behavior through a culturally sensitive lens, one may find that traditional notions of what is "abnormal" and what determines whether an individual has a mental disorder are inadequate (Eriksen & Kress, 2005). When attempting to identify and classify behavior as maladaptive, the ethical counselor will take into consideration social, cultural, and economic factors (Tomlinson-Clarke & Georges, 2014). Being sensitive to the influence of these factors and viewing each client as unique will help counselors make an accurate diagnosis and engage in ethical practice (Swartz-Kulstad & Martin, 1999). The ACA Code of Ethics makes this point quite clear: "Counselors recognize that culture affects the manner in which clients' problems are defined and experienced. Clients' socioeconomic and cultural experiences are considered when diagnosing mental disorders" (ACA 2014, Principle, E.5.b, p. 11).

If we return to the dilemma shared by the counselor at the opening of this chapter, he may have had a different perspective on his student's decision if viewing that decision through a culturally sensitive eye. Understanding her culture, values, and economics may have helped him see that her decision to forgo her scholarships to college in order to work in the family restaurant was congruent with her self-embraced family values and not a manifestation of unhealthy enmeshment or some form of separation anxiety.

The failure of the mental health profession to consider client diversity when identifying and classifying behavior as maladaptive has resulted in the misdiagnosis and overpathologizing of African American, Hispanic, and Latino clients (Johnson, 2013; Sue & Sue, 2013). Given this history of misdiagnosing, the ethical counselor has been directed to "recognize historical and social prejudices in the misdiagnosis and pathologizing of certain individuals and groups and strive to become aware of and address such biases in themselves or others" (ACA, 2014, Principle E.5.c, p. 11).

Beyond the negative impact that a counselor's bias and narrow cultural perspective can have on the identification of a client's "problem," we must be mindful of the inherent bias that has been built into a number of our traditional assessment tools.

> Counselors select and use with caution assessment techniques normed on populations other than that of the client. Counselors recognize the effects of age, color, culture, disability, ethnic group, gender, race, language preference, religion, spirituality, sexual orientation, and socioeconomic status on test administration and interpretation, and they place test results in proper perspective with other relevant factors. (ACA, 2014, Principle E.8, p. 12)

Intervention and Treatment Planning

Just as our assessment and identification of our client's issues must be screened through a lens of multicultural competency, so too must our formulation of intervention plans reflect our awareness of the unique worldview and cultural factors that impact our clients (Robinson & Howard-Hamilton, 2000). While trained in Western psychological theory and empirically supported interventions, the ethical counselor who is engaged with a diverse client population must be aware of the indigenous models of helping and, when appropriate, engage these valued resources in the treatment of the client. Engaging the clients with other culturally responsive and supportive resources and models of helping demonstrates respect for the client as a multidimensional cultural being (Lee & Armstrong, 1995). "Counselors recognize that support networks hold various meanings in the lives of clients and consider enlisting the support, understanding, and involvement of others (e.g., religious/spiritual/community leaders, family members, friends) as positive resources, when appropriate, with client consent" (ACA, 2014, Principle A.1.d, p. 4).

Multicultural Competency: An Ethical "Given"

It may be easy to dismiss the need for development of multicultural competency if one assumes that they will professionally engage only with individuals from the same culture. Such an attitude reflects a narrow view of culture and diversity. As Arredondo (1999) noted, all counseling exists within a context, which is influenced by institutional and societal biases and norms—therefore, counseling is unavoidably a culture-bound profession. Given the fact that their worldviews will shape all interactions between counselor and client, it is incumbent on all ethical counselors to gain the knowledge, personal awareness, sensitivity, dispositions, and skills necessary to be a culturally competent counselor (ACA, 2014, Principle C.2.a).

A multiculturally competent counselor is one who has "self-awareness of values and biases, understand[s] client worldviews, and intervene[s] in a culturally appropriate manner" (Hays, 2008, p. 95). According to the *Association for Multicultural Counseling and Development (AMCD) model of multicultural counseling competencies* (Arrendondo et al., 1996), the ethical counselor is aware of their own cultural beliefs and their level of comfort and sensitivity in working with culturally diverse clients; gains cultural knowledge of the historical and sociopolitical backgrounds of their clients, the family, and community and their psychosocial adjustments; and develops "empathic understanding" of their clients. This ethical requirement to be aware, knowledgeable, and skilled in working with those of different views was expanded by the Multicultural and Social Justice Counseling Competencies (MSJCC; Ratts et al., 2015) to include counselor action in addressing issues of privilege and oppression when working with a wide variety of social identities espoused by clients. The call to action reflects the position that attitudes, beliefs, knowledge, and skills need to be operationalized in action. The MSJCC thus require counseling professionals to see client issues from a culturally contextual framework and recommend interventions that take place at both individual and systems levels (Ratts et al., 2016).

Exercise 4.1 provides a sampling of the MSJCC articulated by Ratts et al. (2015). You are invited to assess your levels of competency and begin to identify a path for professional development.

EXERCISE 4.1

MULTICULTURAL SOCIAL JUSTICE COUNSELING

Directions: The following table identifies the attitudes, knowledge, skills, and actions necessary to engage in competent multicultural social justice counseling. Review the areas of competencies listed and identify those that you feel you possess and those that you feel need to be developed. It would be of value to go to the listing of competencies (see reference at end of chapter) and identify two of the areas where your competency needs to be developed and, perhaps with a colleague or supervisor, identify a plan for your continued professional development.

Multicultural Social Justice Counseling Competencies

	Attitudes, knowledge, skills, and actions	Competency achieved	Competency to be developed
I. Counselor self-awareness	Privileged and marginalized counselors develop self-awareness so that they may explore their attitudes and beliefs and develop knowledge, skills, and action relative to their self-awareness and worldview.		
II. Client worldview	Privileged and marginalized counselors are aware, knowledgeable, skilled, and action oriented in understanding clients' worldview.		
III. Counseling relationship	Privileged and marginalized counselors are aware, knowledgeable, skilled, and action oriented in understanding how client and counselor privileged and marginalized statuses influence the counseling relationship.		
IV. Counseling and advocacy interventions	Privileged and marginalized counselors intervene with and on behalf of clients at the intrapersonal, interpersonal, institutional, community, public policy, and international/global levels.		

Adapted from Ratts et al., 2015.

A Transcultural Approach to Ethical Decision Making

Given the influence of Western values and the Western worldview on the counseling process, and the fact that in some cases this influence is antithetical to a client's worldview, the ethical counselor needs to approach decision making with an expanded, social constructivist view (Cottone, 2001). Operating from a social constructivist orientation, ethical counselors will approach practice decisions from a collaborative, consensual viewpoint, valuing the influence of their own and their clients' worldview (Cottone et al., 2007).

Garcia et al. (2003) have outlined an ethical decision-making model that is transcultural. These authors note that the model is based primarily on the integrative model initially proposed by Tarvydas (1998), with the incorporation of elements of the social constructivism and collaborative models of decision making. The unique cultural elements of this model are found in Table 4.1.

TABLE 4.1. **INCLUDING TRANSCULTURAL ELEMENTS TO ETHICAL DILEMMA RESOLUTION IN COUNSELING**

Step	Transcultural Element
Step 1: Interpreting the situation through awareness and fact finding	When gathering facts about the situation, the counselor should also consider the client's culture as well as the counselor's awareness of their own and the client's cultural identity, acculturation, and role socialization; the counselor should have awareness of their own multicultural counseling competence skills.
Step 2: Formulating an ethical decision	When formulating pathways to ethical decision making, the counselor needs to consider not only professional standards, institutional policies, and laws but the cultural worldview of all involved.
Step 3: Weighing competing, nonmoral values and affirming the course of action	The counselor considers value selection at the cultural level.
Step 4: Planning and executing the selected course of action	In developing and implementing decisions, the counselor not only identifies culturally relevant resources and strategies for the implementation of the plan but also anticipates cultural biases and the countermeasures needed.

Adapted from Garcia et al., 2003, p. 273.

Applying an Ethical Decision-Making Model

The Dilemma

Mrs. Morton, a marriage counselor, was working with Bao and Mai Wang and was caught off guard when at the end of the second session, the couple produced a hand-carved statue as a gift. While Mrs. Morton initially attempted to show appreciation while returning the gift, the couple's insistence was such that she accepted the gift, fearing her further refusal would be insulting to the couple.

Although she decided to take the gift, Mrs. Morton continued to feel uncomfortable with her decision and unsure whether accepting such a gift was a violation of her professional ethics. She engaged the following process to resolve the ethical dilemma in which she found herself.

Identifying the Problem

1. What are the facts of the situation that appear to be contributing to the dilemma? Is the problem personal, clinical, legal, or ethical?
   a. Mr. and Mrs. Wang provided a hand-carved statue as a gift to their counselor.
   b. Mrs. Morton is a licensed mental health counselor and adheres to the ACA Code of Ethics.

2. What is the nature of the problem (personal, clinical, legal, or ethical)?
    a. While initially attempting to show gratitude for the couple's intent while rejecting the gift, Mrs. Morton was concerned that refusing the gift or returning it after having accepted it would be insulting to the couple and negatively impact their therapeutic relationship.
    b. Mrs. Morton was unsure of the possible cultural implications of gift giving for this couple born and raised in Taiwan.

Formulating the Ethical Concern

1. How might the dilemma relate to specific principles listed in the professional code of ethics?
    a. The giving and receiving of gifts appear to extend the relationship beyond traditional professional boundaries (ACA, 2014, Principle A.6.b).
    b. The initial refusal appeared to be received as disrespectful, violating the primary responsibility of counselors to respect the dignity of their clients (ACA, 2014, Principle A.1.a).
2. How might the dilemma relate Mrs. Morton's values, worldview, or personal needs?
    a. Mrs. Morton views gifts as things that are shared between individuals with personal relationships and as signs of affection. She is concerned that if that is the intent of this gift, it is outside the professional nature and boundaries of the relationship.
3. What is the nature and dimension of the dilemma?
    a. The dilemma seems to be primarily one of boundary crossing.
    b. It is hard to assess the potential for harm to the client and the counseling relationship, or the benefit that could be accrued concerning client welfare, regardless of the decision. The initial impression was that rejection of the gift was harmful to the relationship.

Generating Potential Courses of Action

1. Return the gift at the next session with an explanation describing the boundaries of the professional relationship.
2. Keep the gift but discuss the nature of a professional relationship and the desire to not receive gifts in the future.
3. Discuss with the clients their intent and the meaning they hold for such a process of gift giving. If the intent and motivation appear appropriate to the nature of a professional relationship, show gratitude while identifying other forms of expression, such as a simple thank-you, that would be sufficient and in line with both parties' cultural values.

Consulting With a Colleague?

Mrs. Morton contacted a professor from her graduate program, Dr. Zhang, who explained to her that in Chinese culture, gift giving is a sign of respect and gratitude. He also pointed out that it is possible that the couple felt as if they had received a gift from the counselor and were merely reciprocating, which would be part of the culture. Dr. Zhang referred Mrs. Morton to the current ACA Code of Ethics, which does not prohibit counselors from receiving gifts but directs them to consider the nature of the therapeutic relationship, the monetary value of the gift, the client's motivation for giving the gift, and the counselor's motivation for wanting to accept or decline the gift (ACA, 2014, Principle A.10.f).

Assessing Each Option

1. Having accepted the gift, returning it may be perceived as disrespectful and may negatively impact the therapeutic relationship.
2. Accepting the gift without having a conversation about it might indirectly encourage more gift giving.
3. Sharing with the clients the need for and the nature of the professional relationship, while at the same time expressing the counselor's appreciation for the respect and gratitude being conveyed by the client's offering of such a gift.
4. Invite the couple to work collaboratively on identifying alternative nongift forms of gratitude that could be shared by both the counselor and the clients as the relationship continues to develop.

Selecting a Course of Action

1. Mrs. Morton read about the meaning of gift giving in Chinese culture. She discovered that gift giving is often a sign of reciprocity, which in this case would be a reflection of the couple experiencing the counselor's time and work as a "gift" to them. With this as her assumption, she decided to thank the couple for the carving once again but then invite them to reconsider other ways both they and the counselor could share their respect and gratitude for the work they were all doing.

Implementing a Course of Action

1. In the next session, Mrs. Morton shared her new understanding of "gifting," and together, the couple and the counselor decided that a respectful word (e.g., "thank you") or gesture (e.g., prayerful bow) would be sufficient ways of conveying respect and gratitude.

Keystones

- Counselors need to increase their sensitivity and competency with clients of diverse racial and ethnic backgrounds as well as those of different ability status, sexual orientation, socioeconomic status, and spirituality.
- Many of the fundamental "truths" on which we as counselors have based our decisions—"truths" such as the definition of what is "normal," the universality of linear thinking, and our focus on the individual and psychological primacy of independence—are now being reconsidered in light of our understanding of cultural diversity.
- Working within the cross-cultural zone requires a counselor to embrace a broader perspective on culture and recognize that Western-based psychological theory may not directly translate to an application with other cultures.

- When attempting to identify and classify behavior as maladaptive, the ethical counselor will take into consideration social, cultural, and economic factors.
- Counselors must be mindful of the inherent bias that has been built into a number of our traditional assessment tools and use techniques normed on populations other than that of the client with caution.
- In treatment planning, the ethical counselor who is engaged with a diverse client population must be aware of the indigenous models of helping and, when appropriate, engage these valued resources in the treatment of the client.
- Given the fact that their worldviews will shape all interactions between counselor and client, it is incumbent on all ethical counselors to gain the knowledge, personal awareness, sensitivity, dispositions, and skills necessary to be a culturally competent counselor (ACA, 2014, Principle C.2.a).

Additional Resources

Print-Based

Asnaani, A., & Hofmann, S. G. (2012). Collaboration in culturally responsive therapy: Establishing a strong therapeutic alliance across cultural lines. *Journal of Clinical Psychology, 68*(2), 187–197.

Clay, R. (2015). Competence vs. conscience: "Conscience clause" initiatives expand beyond psychology training into the practice arena. *APA Monitor on Psychology, 46*(4), 64.

Durodoye, B. A. (2013). Ethical issues in multicultural counseling. In C. Lee (Ed.), *Multicultural issues in counseling: New approaches to diversity* (4th ed., pp. 295–308). American Counseling Association.

Garrett McAuliffe and Associates. (2012). *Culturally alert counseling: A comprehensive introduction.* SAGE Publications.

Web-Based

American Counseling Association. (2019). Competencies. https://www.counseling.org/knowledge-center/competencies

American Psychological Association. (2014). Guidelines on multicultural education, training, research, practice, and organizational change for psychologists. http://www.apa.org/pi/oema/resources/policy/multicultural-guidelines.aspx

Lebeauf, I. Smaby, M., & Maddux, C. (2009). Adapting counseling skills of multicultural and diverse clients. American Counseling Association. http://www.counseling.org/resources/library/vistas/2009-v-print/Article%204%20LeBeaufSmabyMaddux.pdf

Multicultural and Social Justice Counseling Competencies. http://www.multiculturalcounseling.org/index.php?option=com_content&view=article&id=205:amcd-endorses-multicultural-and-social-justice-counseling-competencies&catid=1:latest&Itemid=123

References

American Counseling Association. (2014). *ACA code of ethics.*

Arredondo, P. (1999). Multicultural competencies as tools to address oppression and racism. *Journal of Counseling and Development, 77,* 102–109.

Arredondo, P., Torporek, R., Brown, S. P., Jones, J., Locke, D. C., Sanchez, J., & Stadler, H. (1996). Operationalization of the multicultural counseling competencies. *Journal of Multicultural Counseling & Development, 24,* 42–78.

Biswas, J., Gangadhar, B. N., & Keshavan, M. (2016). Cross cultural variations in psychiatrists' perception of mental illness: A tool for teaching culture in psychiatry. *Asian J Psychiatry, 23,* 1–7.

Cottone, R. R. (2001). A social constructivism model of ethical and professional issues in counseling. *Journal of Counseling & Development, 79,* 39–45.

Cottone, R. R., Tarvydas, V., & Claus, R. E. (2007). Ethical decision-making processes. In R. R. Cottone & V. M. Tarvydas (Eds.), *Ethical and professional issues in counseling* (3rd ed., pp. 85–113). Education.

Eriksen, K., & Kress, V. (2005). *Beyond the DSM story: Ethical quandaries, challenges, and best practices.* SAGE Publications.

Garcia, J. G., Cartwright, B. W., Stacey, M., & Borzuchowska, B. (2003). A transcultural integrative model for ethical decision making in counseling. *Journal of Counseling & Development, 81(3),* 268–277.

Glosoff, H. L., & Kocet, M. M. (2006). Highlights of the 2005 ACA Code of Ethics. In G. R. Walz, J. Bleuer, & R. K. Yep (Eds.), VISTAS: Compelling perspectives on counseling, 2006 (pp. 5-9). Alexandria, VA: American Counseling Association.

Hankivsky, O., & Cormier, R. (2009). *Intersectionality: Moving women's health research and policy forward.* Women's Health Research Network. http://bccewh.bc.ca/wp-content/uploads/2012/05/2009_IntersectionaliyMoving-womenshealthresearchandpolicyforward.pdf

Hays, D. G. (2008). Assessing multicultural competence in counselor trainees: A review of instrumentation and future directions. *Journal of Counseling & Development, 86,* 95–101.

Hernandez, M., Nesman, T., Mowery, D., Acevedo-Polakovich, I. D., Callejas, L. M. (2009). Cultural competence: A literature review and conceptual model for mental health services. *Psychiatric Services 60,* 1046–1050.

Johnson, R. (2013). Forensic and culturally responsive approach for the DSM-5: Just the FACTS. *Journal of Theory Construction & Testing, 17,* 18–22.

Kaplan, D. M., Kocet, M. M., Cottone, R. R., Glosoff, H. L., Miranti, J. G., Moll, E. C., Bloom, W., Bringaze, T. B., Herlihy, B., Lee, C. C., & Tarvydas, V. M. (2009). New mandates and imperatives in the revised ACA Code of Ethics. *Journal of Counseling & Development, 87,* 241–256.

Kaplan, D. M., Tarvydas, V. M., & Gladding, S. T. (2013). *20/20: A vision for the future of counseling: The new consensus definition of counseling.* http://www.counseling.org/docs/david-kaplan's-files/consensusdefinition-of-counseling.docx?sfvrsn=2

Lee, C. C., & Armstrong, K. L. (1995). Indigenous models of mental health interventions. In J. C. Ponterroto, J. M. Casas, L. A. Suzuki, & C. M. Alexander (Eds.), *Handbook of multicultural counseling* (pp. 441–456). SAGE Publications.

Lugo Steidel, A., & Contreras, J. M. (2003). A new familism scale for use with Latino populations. *Hispanic Journal of Behavioral Sciences, 25,* 312–330.

Marsella, A. J. (2011). Twelve critical issues for mental health professionals working with ethnoculturally diverse populations. *Psychology International, 2011*(22), 7–10. http://www.apa.org/international/pi/2011/10/critical-issues.aspx

Nguyen, D., & Bornheimer, L. A. (2014). Mental health service use types among Asian Americans with a psychiatric disorder: Considerations of culture and need. *The Journal of Behavioral Health Services & Research, 41*, 520–528.

Ratts, M. J., Singh. A. A., Nassar-McMillan, S., Kent Butler, S., & Rafferty McCullough, J. (2015). Multicultural and social justice counseling competencies. https://www.counseling.org/docs/default-source/competencies/multicultural-and-social-justice-counseling-competencies.pdf?sfvrsn=20

Ratts, M. J., Singh. A. A., Nassar-McMillan, S., Kent Butler, S., Rafferty McCullough, J. (2016). Multicultural and social justice counseling competencies: Practical application in counseling. https://ct.counseling.org/2016/01/multicultural-and-social-justice-counseling-competencies-practical-applications-in-counseling/

Robinson, T. L., & Howard-Hamilton, M. F. (2000). *The convergence of race, ethnicity, and gender: Multiple identities in counseling.* Merrill.

Sue, D. W., & Sue, D. (1999). *Counseling the culturally different: Theory and practice.* Wiley.

Sue, D. W., & Sue, D. (2013). *Counseling the culturally diverse: Theory and practice* (6th ed.). Wiley.

Swartz-Kulstad, J. L., & Martin, W. E. (1999). Impact of culture and context on psychosocial adaptation: The cultural and contextual guide process. *Journal of Counseling & Development, 77*, 281–293.

Tarvydas, V.M. (1998). Ethical decision-making processes. In R.R. Cottone & V.M. Tarvydas (Eds.), *Ethical and Professional Issues in Counseling* (pp. 144–154). Upper Saddle River, NJ: Prentice Hall.

Tomlinson-Clarke, S. M., & Georges, C. M. (2014). "DSM-5": A commentary on integrating multicultural and strength-based considerations into counseling training and practice. *Professional Counselors, 4*(3), 272–281.

U.S. Department of Health and Human Services. (2001). *Mental health: Culture, race, and ethnicity: A supplement to mental health: A report of the surgeon general.*

Chapter 5

Client and Context

I know what we're usually supposed to do, but what about when …

COUNSELORS ARE INHERENTLY "generalist practitioners." They possess core knowledge and skills that can be applied with a diverse clientele in a variety of settings. This strong foundation of knowledge and skill also allows them to adapt their approach to meet the unique needs of their unique clients. Much is the same from an ethical perspective. Our ethical codes provide the core foundation of ethical practices, regardless of context. As mentioned in previous chapters, however, those ethical codes allow for a great deal of gray area for the counselor to interpret. Thus, when working with complex populations in various settings and contexts, there is an expectation that counselors will factor in the unique nature of each case when navigating those gray ethical areas.

This chapter introduces a selection of unique populations and contexts that the 21st-century counselor is likely to encounter in their work. After completing this chapter, readers will be able to

1. identify common populations and settings/contexts where the application of counseling ethics may be more complex,
2. identify the gray areas in those unique cases and explain how the customary/literal interpretation of the related ethical codes may or may not apply, and
3. explain how existing ethical codes may be interpreted/applied to fit the needs of the unique populations and contexts covered.

Client Served

Each time a new client walks through your door, they redefine the landscape of your professional process. Their issues (e.g., depression) may be common, and the rules (e.g., ethical codes) may remain the same. Yet the unique nature of that client will have an undeniable impact on how the counselor approaches the case. It is like painting the same picture but with a new palette of colors to choose from. Just as some colors naturally blend and others do not, some legal and ethical mandates are easily applied to a client while others are more complex.

Minors

Counseling minors is perhaps one of the most complex endeavors from an ethical perspective. Regardless of the client, the counselor is compelled to provide client care in accordance with the same ethical code. As you will see in the upcoming paragraphs, however, the ways in which a counselor honors those ethical obligations can change dramatically. Factor in the legal mandates that do not always parallel their ethical counterparts and you are left with a number of professional expectations that can be seemingly mutually exclusive (Orton, 1997).

Counseling is an inherently contractual relationship. As such, it can only exist in the purview of the law. In creating that legally binding relationship, counselors accept the fiduciary duty (Ludes & Gilbert, 1998), to put the client's needs above their own. It also compels the counselor and client to define roles, responsibilities, expectations, and so on. This should sound very familiar to what we know as our ethical obligation to secure informed consent (ACA, 2014, Standard A.2.a). When treating a minor, however, these seemingly compatible legal and ethical obligations diverge.

Minors inherently lack the capacity to enter into a contractual relationship. Thus, counseling can only be provided to a minor with the authorization of a legal guardian. A contractual relationship is still formed, but it is between the counselor and the minor's legal representative. In addition to this legal obligation to the employer (e.g., the parent), counselors also assume an ethical obligation to the minor client. What happens when those obligations compete with one another?

Counselors are provided with some guidance in such situations by Standard A.2.d., Inability to Give Consent (APA, 2014). This standard recognizes the need to meet legal requirements but also suggests incorporating the client, in this case the minor, meaningfully into the consent process. Although not legally binding, counselors can still request the minor client's *assent* and incorporate them into the decision-making process whenever possible. Doing so would also honor, in a minor key, the client's autonomy, which is one of the core principles of professional ethical behavior (ACA, 2014). As future sections will illustrate, however, this may not necessarily prevent all legal and ethical issues when working with minors.

It is worth mentioning here that historically, individuals in the United States have been granted adult status at age 18 and along with it the capacity to enter into a contractual relationship such as with a counselor. In response to the growing complexities of mental health issues in children, certain states have begun adopting laws that allow minors limited rights to enter into a counseling relationship independently and without the consent of a parent (e.g., NJ Rev Stat § 9:17A-4 (2013)). Since these limited rights may differ across states, practitioners are advised to research the laws of the land in which they practice.

Another common ethical issue that arises when working with minors is that of confidentiality. Confidentiality is a linchpin to the counseling relationship (ACA, 2014). Without it, effective counseling is impossible. The law also recognizes the importance of confidentiality, with some states granting clients privileged communication rights. How confidentiality while working with minors becomes an issue is also related to the contractual nature of counseling.

Standard B.1.c. of the ACA Code of Ethics states, "Counselors protect the confidential information of prospective and current clients. Counselors disclose information only with appropriate consent or with sound legal or ethical justification" (ACA, 2014, p. 7). As stated earlier, contracts when counseling minors exist between the counselor and the legal guardian who consents to treatment. Therefore, our *legal* obligations to protect client information belong to the guardian, who determines what the nature and scope of that confidentiality should be. Yet confidentiality is a cornerstone of the counseling *relationship*, which in this case exists between the counselor and minor client. It is to that relationship that we as counselors are ethically bound. What then is the appropriate action when our legal justification for breaking confidentiality conflicts with our ethical justification? Consider the challenges to maintaining confidentiality found in the following case illustration (Case Illustration 5.1).

CASE ILLUSTRATION 5.1

TO TELL OR NOT TO TELL

Tracey is a 16-year-old female who was enrolled in counseling by her parents. Tracey's parents stated that they have observed an increase in worrisome behavior. She has violated curfew consistently over the past month, and when her parents took away her "going out privileges," she snuck out of the house. Tracey's parents also stated that she has been dressing more provocatively over the past 6 months and that they are particularly worried she is inviting the wrong kind of attention from boys. When you met with Tracey, she admitted to missing curfew, stating, "I don't have a car and I feel stupid riding a bike, so I walk." She also admitted to sneaking out of the house, stating, "I was 15 minutes late and they told me I couldn't go to the football game. They knew I wanted to go see my friend Sarah cheer." When asked about her dress, Tracey stated, "They think if I'm not wearing church clothes that I'm 'showing too much skin.' They almost didn't let me wear this today to see you." Tracey seemed appropriately dressed at the time.

In your most recent session with Tracey, she admitted that she snuck out of the house again over the weekend. She stated that her friend Kenny asked her to come watch him play. She is considering sneaking out with her friend Sarah to watch Kenny play again next week. She asks you to promise not to tell her parents. You know that her parents would want to be informed.

Are you obligated to tell the parents?

- If not, why?
- If so, where does that obligation come from?

In this case we see an obvious disconnect between our legal and ethical obligations. It is important to remember in such situations that neither our personal nor ethical position supersedes the law. Later in the chapter, we will outline a more detailed application of an ethical decision-making model to resolve this hypothetical scenario. As with most issues, however, prevention is preferred over remediation. It is that position that the ACA Code of Ethics outlines more definitively. Standard B.1.d., which stipulates, "At initiation and throughout the counseling process, counselors inform clients of the limitations of confidentiality and seek to identify situations in which confidentiality must be breached" (ACA, 2014, p. 7). When working with minors, it will be particularly important to define the nature of those limitations during the informed *assent* process. The counselor may also take that opportunity to educate the client's parent or guardian on the importance of confidentiality and the impact it has on the counselor's ability to provide effective care.

When Competence Is Challenged

As described previously, minors are considered to be lacking in the capacity to consent to a contractual relationship with a client. Much in the same way, adult clients may be diagnosed with some sort of developmental or cognitive impairment that impacts their capacity to consent to services. In such cases, consent is typically provided by the prospective client's conservator, a person appointed by a court to serve as the "incompetent" individual's legal representative (Ahia, 2009). By engaging in this contractual relationship with the client's conservator, all of the issues described above when counseling a minor (e.g., informed consent, confidentiality) are created. In the same way, all of the above prescriptions (e.g., obtaining client assent) can be applied in cases such as these. A unique challenge that may arise here relates back to how the scope of one's "incompetence" is defined. According to Ahia (2009), persons can be declared generally incompetent and unable to make *any* critical legal decisions or incompetent only as it relates to a single civil right or privilege. How then are counselors to determine the capacity of their client to consent to services?

CASE ILLUSTRATION 5.2

DEFINING CAPACITY

Ben is a 36-year-old male who schedules an intake session with you at your private practice. During his intake, Ben states that he is relatively new to the area and is seeking a new counselor. According to Ben, he has been receiving counseling regularly over the past 4 years and was initially diagnosed with schizotypal personality disorder. He reports that he has been consistently stable over the past 4 years. His speech pattern is somewhat awkward but mostly easy to understand. His dress and affect are unremarkable. When the intake interview turned to questions about finances and payment, Ben stated that his sister would handle any bills. "The judge gave her control of my money a few years ago when I went a little loopy. That was before I started counseling. I could probably get it back now but she's good at financial stuff and it's one less thing for me worry about."

- Does Ben have the capacity to initiate a counseling relationship?
- What additional information could you collect to help you determine his competence?

In this illustration, we see how the scope of competence may vary from one privilege to the next. Being deemed incompetent as it relates to financial independence may not necessarily indicate that an individual is unable to consent to counseling services. In the absence of any definitive legal declaration of the client's competence, the counselor is left to make their own assessment based on the facts presented, observations, and any additional information they can acquire.

Mandated Clients

Mandated clients represent another unique population from a legal and ethical perspective. In cases of mandated counseling, some entity with authority (e.g., the court system) stipulates that the party in question either engages in counseling services or suffers some type of consequence (e.g., jail). As opposed to the populations described earlier, obtaining consent is not necessarily an issue. This may seem counterintuitive, being that clients are "mandated," but that term is somewhat misleading. As opposed to an individual being "mandated" in accordance with the traditional definition of the word, "mandated clients" do have an option to refuse service. Doing so would simply come with specific consequences. In that way, clients are not mandated as much as they are begrudging participants. Regardless, unique ethical issues are created when working with this population (Kiracofe & Wells, 2007).

As was the case above, (Case Illustration 5.2) one of the most significant issues when working with this population revolves around confidentiality. When an individual is mandated to counseling, that mandate is almost always accompanied by some sort of requirement to report back to the entity in charge. The scope of this report can vary greatly. Whereas in one scenario a counselor may only need to confirm the client's attendance record, in another the counselor may need to provide specific and regular progress reports. Regardless of scope, these reports are likely to be a nonnegotiable element of the client's mandated care, should they choose to participate. This inherently creates unique limitations to confidentiality that can have a significant impact on the counseling relationship.

In this case, the counselor may not believe that the client's disclosure was an indication that they are a current flight risk. But the counselor has not however been empowered to make such a determination and thus could be compelled to share this information in their report, regardless of the relevance to the client's current care or the negative impact it could have on the client's status in the facility or the counseling relationship.

Being that mandated clients still willingly consent to treatment, they are entitled to be "informed" just as any other client would be at the onset of treatment. In these unique cases, however, counselors should feel compelled to include in that informed consent process a discussion about the limits to confidentiality as it relates to any reports or evaluations the counselor is mandated to provide. In doing so, the client can more deliberately select what information they provide during sessions.

CASE ILLUSTRATION 5.3

BEGRUDGING PARTICIPANT

Anne is an 18-year-old female currently residing in a juvenile detention center. She was detained at the juvenile center after being caught shoplifting and assaulting a security guard when confronted. She has been at the center for 4 months and is set to be released early for good behavior. In your most recent session with her, Anne shared that during a friend's visit to the center a few weeks ago, she found out her boyfriend had been cheating on her while she was locked up. She said, "He's lucky I couldn't get out of here." With more probing into her statement, Anne admitted that she stole a butter knife from the cafeteria and smuggled it back to her room. "I didn't know what I was doing," she said. "I fiddled around at the door lock for a bit and then gave up." When asked what her intentions were at the time, Anne stated, "I don't know. It's not like I could have gotten out of here even if the door did open. All I could think about was just getting out of here so I could find him and smack him across the face." Anne stated that she returned the butter knife to the cafeteria the next day and never attempted any similar actions. When asked if she'd see her ex-boyfriend after she was released, she stated, "Hell no. I didn't spend all this time in here just to get out and waste my time with him. I have better things to do with my life."

- Anne has clearly broken the rule of the facility. Should you report it?
- What are the consequences of reporting Anne's behavior?
- What are the consequences of not reporting Anne's behavior?

Context and Setting

What has been described up to this point are specific legal and ethical issues that are created by the inherent nature of certain populations. It is worth mentioning that similar issues may be created, not due to any specific client characteristic, but instead due to the nature of the system or setting in which the client is being treated. Much in the same way counselors should educate themselves on the state laws that dictate their practices, they should also stay informed about the policies in their systems.

School systems continue to be one of the more complex settings for counselors to practice. In addition to the unique challenges of working with minors, not only are school counselors obligated to the laws of the land and the ethics of the profession, they are also governed by the policies of the school. While it could be argued that since school counseling is a "regular" educational service, school counselors would not need parental permission to provide counseling to students, it must be noted that parents hold the final say and can specifically forbid a counselor to work with their minor student. Therefore, it is important for school counselors or those working in the school setting with minor students to check school policy and state and federal laws regarding the need to gain parental consent before working with minor students. These three governing bodies may not always be in alignment.

CASE ILLUSTRATION 5.4

INFORMING THE PARENTS?

Becka is a 16-year-old student who you have seen off and on since she was assigned to your caseload at Bird Feather High School. She performs relatively well in classes and has had no disciplinary issues beyond occasionally being assigned detention after texting in class. She visited you in your office this week and requested an impromptu meeting. During this meeting, Becka disclosed that she was pregnant. She stated that she and her boyfriend had sex for the first time not long before and that she was only 5 weeks along. When you asked her plan, she stated that she still didn't know whether she wanted to keep the baby and had picked up a pamphlet about abortions from a local Planned Parenthood center. She begged you not to tell her parents so she could have time to figure things out. The district in which Bird Feather High is housed does not have a policy to immediately report pregnancies to parents, but one has just recently been proposed.

- What are your responsibilities in this case, legally, ethically, and professionally?

In this case we can see the potential intersection of law, ethics, and system policy. Although some helping professionals are of the opinion that rigid policies do a potential disservice to students and their counselors (Stone, 2012), many districts have moved forward with adopting the policy to immediately report to parents cases such as Becka's. In cases such as *Port Washington Teachers' Association v. Board of Education of the Port Washington Union Free School District* (2007), courts have upheld the right of school districts to implement such policies, which would also suggest that said polices are not unlawful. From an ethical perspective, school counselors must often assess student behaviors to determine whether there is sufficient risk to warrant breaking confidentiality (Moyer & Sullivan, 2008). It has been argued, however, that a teen pregnancy does not inherently come with any foreseeable danger to the teen or others (Ciciora, 2010). And as described in previous sections, counselors tend to lean toward maintaining confidentiality whenever possible.

Schools are not the only systems that create new layers of consideration when it comes to ethics. The section on mandated clients outlined some of the moving parts of providing care in the justice system. Consider now working with clients within a substance abuse rehabilitation facility. Many such facilities provide inpatient care, during which participants are required to refrain from any sort of substance use. Violations of such a policy could jeopardize the client's status in the program. Consider providing services to such a client who eventually discloses that they have been actively using while staying at the facility. From an ethical perspective, we want to honor the client's right to confidentiality. Counselors also consider the principle of nonmaleficence, or "do no harm," when providing care to clients, and involuntary termination of services due to violating agency policies is likely to have a negative impact on the client when they find themselves without support.

Keystones

- Counseling is an inherently contractual relationship, one that can only exist in the purview of the law. This fact calls into question the ability of minors or those with limited competency to enter into such a contractual relationship.

- The interpretation and application of ethical codes can change significantly based on the counselor, the population being served, or the system/agency in which services are being provided.

- Although not legally binding, counselors can still request a minor client's *assent* and incorporate them into the decision-making process whenever possible.

- For those working with "mandated" clients, the ethical directive to respect the autonomy of the client remains intact; clients, even those designated as "mandated," are free to refuse service and entitled to be "informed" just as any other client would be at the onset of treatment.

- The nature of the system or setting in which the client is being treated can also give form to the procedures required to establish an ethical counseling relationship. Counselors should not only educate themselves on the state and federal laws that dictate their practices but also stay informed about the policies in their systems.

Additional Resources

Print-Based

Issacs, M. L., & Stone, C. (2001). Confidentiality with minors: Mental health counselors' attitudes toward breaching or preserving confidentiality. *Journal of Mental Health Counseling, 23*(4), 342–356.

Schmidt, J. J. (2003). Counseling in schools: Essential services and comprehensive programs (4th ed.). Allyn & Bacon.

Snyder, C. M. J., & Anderson, S. A. (2009). An examination of mandated versus voluntary referral as a determinant of clinical outcome. *Journal of Marital and Family Therapy, 35*(3), 278–292.

Sotero, L., Major, S., Escudero, V., & Relvas, A. P. (2016). The therapeutic alliance with clients: How does it work? *Journal of Family Therapy, 38*(1), 36–58.

Wittouck, C., & Vander Beken, T. (2019). Recovery, desistance, and the role of procedural justice in working alliances with mentally ill offenders: A critical review. *Addiction Research & Theory, 27*(1), 16–28.

Web-Based

Lazovsky, R. (2008). Maintaining confidentiality with minors: Dilemmas of school counselors. *Professional School Counseling.* https://doi.org/10.1177/2156759X0801100507

References

Ahia, C. E. (2009). *Legal and ethical dictionary for mental health professionals* (2nd ed.). University Press of America.

American Counseling Association. (2014). *ACA code of ethics*.

Ciciora, P. (2010, June). When a minor becomes pregnant, must schools notify the parents? *Illinois News Bureau*. https://news.illinois.edu/view/6367/198696

Kiracofe, N. M., & Wells, L. (2007). Mandated disciplinary counseling on campus: Problems and possibilities. *Journal of Counseling and Development, 77*, 14–17.

Ludes, F. J., & Gilbert, H. J. (1998). Fiduciary. *Corpus Juris Secundum, 36A*, 381–389.

Moyer, M., & Sullivan, J. (2008). Student risk-taking behaviors: When do school counselors break confidentiality? *Professional School Counseling, 11*, 236–245.

NJ Rev Stat § 9:17A-4 (2013)—Consent by minor to treatment.

Orton, G. L. (1997). *Strategies for counseling with children and their parents*. Brooks/Cole.

Port Washington Teachers' Association v. Board of Education of the Port Washington Union Free School District 478 F.3d 494 (2nd Cir. 2007).

Stone, D. (2012, September). District policy and student pregnancy. *ASCA School Counselor*. https://www.school-counselor.org/magazine/blogs/september-october-2012/district-policy-and-student-pregnancy

Chapter 6

Boundaries

*I genuinely don't know what to do. I opened my Facebook page and
I saw a request from my client—to "friend" her.*

It is obvious even to the newest member of the profession that it is unethical to "hang out" socially with a client. Establishing and maintaining clear boundaries in the counseling relationship is challenging, even when services are provided in person and in a traditional office structure and working hours. These challenges become magnified when digital technology is included in the equation.

The current chapter discusses the nature of and need for professional boundaries, as well as the unique challenges to the establishment and maintenance of boundaries in counseling with a counselor's entry into the digital age. After completing this chapter, readers will be able to

1. describe the role and function of boundaries in a counseling relationship;
2. explain the difference between boundary crossing and boundary violation;
3. explain the differences between dual relationships that are unethical and those that are not; and
4. describe the ethical challenges for counselors' use of emails, text messaging, and social media.

Boundaries—What and Why

Counseling is first and foremost a relationship. Counseling shares many of the characteristics of other close interpersonal relationships. Counseling involves individuals who come to the encounter with personal needs. It is a relationship in which norms or rules governing behavior are developed. However, counseling is unique among close relationships.

Counseling is often an encounter that involves deep personal disclosure and the experience of intense emotions. It is quite often a very intimate encounter. However, unlike other such emotional and intimate relationships, counseling is a relationship wherein only one participant, the client, engages at such a deeply personal level of sharing in hopes of satisfying their needs. While the counselor also enters this relationship with personal needs, these are not the focus of the encounter, nor should they be. Counselors are directed to be driven by one primary need—the need to promote the welfare of the client (ACA, 2014, Standard A.1.a).

Given the very intimate nature of the counseling relationship and the vulnerability of clients, the establishment and maintenance of rules defining the roles to be assumed and the behaviors that are appropriate (as well as inappropriate) is essential. Boundaries define the expected and accepted psychological and social distance between counselors and clients. Boundaries establish that space separating the client and their emotional needs from the counselor and their emotional needs (Kitchener & Anderson, 2011).

Boundaries set limits that are integral to professional effectiveness (Everett & Gallop, 2001). Boundaries help the client and counselor regulate their behavior in ways that maximize therapeutic outcomes and minimize harm (Borys, 1994; Zur, 2007). Boundaries encompass issues such as who the client is, what the payment will be, where and when counseling will take place, when it may be necessary to break confidentiality, how to manage multiple relationships, and issues surrounding termination (Smith & Fitzpatrick, 1995). In establishing the boundaries for a counseling relationship, the counselor establishes what types of interactions are acceptable, clarifies issues related to counselor self-disclosure, and explains issues related to proximity, or the physical distance between client and therapist (Gottlieb et al., 2009; Gutheil & Gabbard, 1993; Zur, 2007).

Boundaries—Dynamic

Because each counseling relationship is unique, colored by the nature of the issue being addressed and the characteristics of the participants, boundaries cannot be rigidly defined or created in a formulaic way. Boundaries need to be adjusted not just between clients but even within a single counseling relationship. Issues of proximity, for example, will certainly differ when working with an adult as opposed to a child. Similarly, proximity boundaries may be adjusted within a counseling interaction in response to the unique needs of the client at any given moment. Navigating the creation and adjustment of boundaries can result in a counselor's variance from standard or traditional roles and functions, and it is often in this deviation that ethical dilemmas may arise.

Boundary issues that have been known to arise in traditional settings include those related to place and space, time, money, role, gifts, physical touch, language, clothing, self-disclosure, and sexual contact (Gutheil & Gabbard, 1993). While any such variance could indicate a boundary concern, a distinction has been made between those deviations that result in client exploitation (i.e., boundary violation) and those that, while nonprofessional, are nonexploitative (i.e., boundary crossing).

Boundary Violation

Boundary violations refer to the egregious and harmful transgressions of the counseling relationship that represent exploitation of the client's vulnerable position. A boundary violation occurs when a counselor misuses their power to exploit a client for the counselor's benefit. Boundary violations are always unethical and are likely to be illegal (Zur, 2018).

Quite often, incidents of boundary violation have been tied to sexual contact between counselors and their clients. Such intimacy between counselor and client is unethical. The ACA Code of Ethics makes no doubt about this, noting, "Sexual and/or romantic counselor–client interactions or relationships with current clients, their romantic partners, or their family members are prohibited" (ACA, 2014, Standard A.5.a).

The potential misuse of power on the part of the counselor, with the potential to harm a client when engaging in sexual and/or romantic relationships, is so concerning that this form of interaction is prohibited even between counselors and former clients for several years after the counseling relationship ends. "Sexual and/or romantic counselor–client interactions or relationships with former clients, their romantic partners, or their family members are prohibited for a period of 5 years following the last professional contact" (ACA, 2014, Standard A.5.c).

While engaging in sexual or romantic contact with one's client is on its face a clear violation of professional boundaries, other forms of boundary violations may be less obvious and yet just as destructive to the welfare of the client. Actions that may at first appear innocuous may later be seen as potential boundary violations if viewed through a lens of "whose needs are being met and at whose expense?" Case Illustration 6.1 depicts a nonsexual boundary violation.

CASE ILLUSTRATION 6.1

I AM HAPPY TO EXTEND YOU CREDIT

Doreen came to counseling following the abrupt ending of her marriage of 6 years. At the time of intake, Doreen presented as mildly depressed and anxious. She explained that she felt isolated, having moved more than 2,000 miles from her family. The move was motivated by the fact that her husband took a new job. She shared that she had not developed any friends in this new location and felt totally "alone" at this time of crisis.

The counselor disclosed that he understood the difficulty adjusting to a new area, since he had also recently moved to this area in order to establish his practice. He "congratulated" Doreen on being his first, and currently only, client.

When discussing fee structure, Doreen explained that she was not employed and that her insurance provided for only eight counseling visits. The counselor explained that this would not be a problem, since he was more than willing to extend her credit, noting, "Something like this could take quite a few weekly sessions to resolve." Doreen expressed her gratitude, stating, "You really are my only support—so I appreciate your willingness to work with me."

FOR REFLECTION AND DISCUSSION

1. How might the adjustment in the fee schedule invite boundary violation and transference (or countertransference)?
2. How might the adjustment in the fee schedule conflict with the values underlying our code of ethics?

It could be argued that the counselor in the case illustration was merely reflecting a desire to assist the client and remove what might be a financial barrier to that assistance. However, given the "newness" of his practice and the absence of other clients, one might question the motivation for his willingness to ensure a long-term contract. Further, given Doreen's sense of social isolation and the absence of family or other social supports, fostering her dependency on the counselor might be another adverse outcome of such an action.

When questioning whether a deviation from traditional counselor behavior and mode of operation constitutes a boundary violation, the focus needs to be on whose need is being met and at whose cost. When the answer is the counselor's needs are being met at the client's costs or negative impact, then a boundary violation has occurred. Table 6.1 provides a brief sampling of nonsexual boundary violations. As you review the situations presented, consider the possible negative impact of these actions on the client.

TABLE 6.1. A SAMPLING OF NONSEXUAL BOUNDARY VIOLATIONS

- Extending the therapeutic contract beyond the point of goal achievement in order to maintain counselor income.
- Encouraging the client to expand on the details of a personal experience in order to satisfy the counselor's prurient needs.
- Continuing a session beyond the scheduled time because the counselor is finding the client's sharing entertaining and enjoys the "company" of the client.
- Scheduling sessions to meet outside of the office without a clear therapeutic rationale or relevance to the treatment plan.
- Soliciting expensive gifts or services from the client.
- Using client knowledge or skills for counselor benefit, as might be the case with a counselor using the session to gain stock advice from a broker.
- Nonsexual physical contact (e.g., a hug, a touch) when initiated by the counselor.

Boundary Crossing

Not all deviations from the traditional mode of operation constitute an ethical violation. While any variation should be taken only after careful consideration of the risk and benefits to the client and the therapeutic relationship, those that are brief, harmless, and nonexploitative of the client would be considered boundary crossings. Such boundary crossing is not automatically viewed as unethical and thus is not automatically prohibited under the counselors' code of ethics (Zur, 2018). Consider the example of a counselor attending a church social only to find that a client is also in attendance.

The social gathering would invite the counselor to move beyond their professional role and prescribed set of professional behaviors. Such a deviation, while not automatically assumed to be harmful to the client, does demand a real sensitivity and adaptability on the part of the counselor. Ignoring the client or attempting to appear not to recognize the client would not only be dishonest but could be misperceived by the client as rejection and thus would be harmful to the relationship. Similarly, imposing oneself on the client or interjecting oneself into the client's conversation would also be potentially embarrassing and harmful to the client.

While there is no prescription on how to handle such a situation, taking the lead from the client on how they wish to engage may be an excellent first step. Allowing the client to initiate contact, make any introductions, or provide some behavioral sign that avoidance is preferred may be the best course of action for the counselor in this situation.

There are circumstances, such as living and working in a small community, that elevate the chances of encountering a client outside of the office. It might be expected that a counselor may need services that the client provides, as would be the case with a counselor who needs automotive repair when the client is the only factory-authorized mechanic in the area. When it comes to boundary crossing, it is essential for counselors to "take appropriate professional precautions such as informed consent, consultation, supervision, and documentation to ensure that judgment is not impaired, and no harm occurs" (ACA, 2014, Standard A.6.b).

As a general rule, it is safe to say that boundary crossing should be minimized if not eliminated. However, there are times and circumstances in which deviating from the traditional patterns of client–counselor interaction can be consciously imposed as support to treatment (Zur, 2001; Lazarus & Zur, 2002). Table 6.2 provides examples of activities and counselor–client interactions that go beyond the traditional framework of a counseling relationship yet are intended to serve the welfare of the client.

TABLE 6.2. **VARIATIONS IN SERVICE OF TREATMENT**

Action	Counselor Considerations	Impact on Client
A counselor spent a morning with the client at a very busy community park.	The counselor was attempting to employ natural exposure to people walking dogs as a way of assisting the client with their PTSD following a dog attack.	The client, while initially reporting being anxious at a 10 (on a scale of 1 to 10, with 10 being the highest), after 40 minutes in the park was able to pet a small dog that a person was walking.
A counselor brought pizza to share with the client.	The client is an adolescent with extreme social anxiety. The counselor hoped that the pizza would provide a focus that reduced the anxiety that results from one-on-one contact.	While initially withdrawn, the client not only took a piece of pizza but requested a second. In the process of this "chat-n-chew" (a term the counselor introduced) session, the client began to more freely disclose and was less withdrawn than during the previous session or the opening of the current session.

Action	Counselor Considerations	Impact on Client
A counselor met the client for lunch at a local restaurant.	The client has an eating disorder and the counselor, taking a behavioral approach, wanted to model and selectively reinforce the client's healthy eating behaviors.	The client, while initially struggling, was able to set small goals, with the help of the counselor and was able to complete a well-balanced, healthy lunch.
A counselor accepted an invitation to the client's child's bat mitzvah.	The counselor and client were nearing termination, and the counselor was concerned that rejection of the invitation might damage what was an excellent therapeutic alliance. The counselor discussed their comfort with attending the service but explained they would not feel as comfortable participating in the celebration that followed.	The client was very appreciative of the counselor's attendance at the service and understood that the counselor would not be attending the family party afterward.
A counselor drove the client to their mother's gravesite.	The counselor felt that standing at the site might help the client move past their resistance to grieving and provide the stimulus needed to facilitate the client's grieving process.	The client found the experience cathartic at the moment, and it positioned them to begin working on their grief in the upcoming sessions.

A Slippery Slope?

As noted, boundary crossing is not automatically unethical. It is essential, however, for counselors to be very aware of their motives and behaviors when extending a boundary outside of the traditional structure. It is possible that what started as an innocuous boundary crossing takes shape in such a way that causes harm to the client or the therapeutic relationship. Under these circumstances, what was a boundary crossing may slide into a boundary violation. Exercise 6.1 invites you to "consult" with a colleague or classmate regarding some atypical contacts between counselor and client. The task is to identify how these boundary crossings may, while benefiting the counselor, slide into harming the client and thus become boundary violations.

EXERCISE 6.1

CROSSING OR VIOLATION?

Directions: Below are some nonprofessional contacts between a counselor and a client. Your task is to identify how this boundary crossing could slide into a boundary violation. The first situation is provided as an illustration.

Scenario	Counselor Motivation	Actions that Could Result in Harm to a Client
(*A Sample Illustration*) A counselor is attending a charity dinner theater. All participants are to "interrogate" the various actors as suspects in a murder case. The counselor is surprised to see their client as one of the main suspects in the portrayed crime.	To impress the other participants with the counselor's ability to analyze the situation and solve the case.	Using their knowledge of the client's marital difficulties, the counselor poses questions to the client-as-suspect that focus on their envy of the "suspect's" marriage.
	To entertain the participants and appear quick-witted.	The counselor uses a very sarcastic tone when questioning the client-as-suspect.
A counselor's general practitioner refers them to a chiropractor for treatment of a lower back problem. The only chiropractor in the area is also the counselor's client.	To demonstrate that they are in top physical shape, the counselor selects clothing that is tight fitting.	
	To appear in full control and nonanxious, the counselor engages in extensive personal disclosure about the injuries that have resulted in the back problem.	
A counselor is participating in a pickup game of basketball at their local YMCA. Their client enters the gym and is invited to join the game.	To win and to demonstrate personal skills, the counselor plays aggressively on defense.	
	To protect the client's ego, the counselor backs off on playing defense when the client has the ball or is taking a shot.	
A counselor stops in a local tavern for a sandwich and a beer. Entering, the counselor realizes that their server is their new client.	To impress the client-server with their generosity, the counselor leaves an excessive 40% gratuity.	
	In hopes of avoiding an uncomfortable interaction, the counselor moves from the booth in which they were sitting to the bar.	

Boundary Challenges in the 21st Century

Counselors and the counselor–client relationship are not immune to the changing norms of the new digital culture (Balick, 2012; Sude, 2013; Zilberstein, 2015). The use of social media, email, and texting introduces additional challenges to ethical practice, including issues of confidentiality, record maintenance, and as is the focus of this chapter, boundaries.

Social Media and "Friending"

Similarly to the counselor whose dilemma opened this chapter; counselors increasingly find themselves in the grasp of an ethical dilemma upon receiving a Facebook friend request. Engaging in electronic contact with a client or former client on a social networking site can blur boundaries, creating a dual relationship and even potentially compromising the client's privacy and confidentiality (Zur, 2018). However, choosing to reject a client's friending request can inadvertently cause the client to feel rejected (Zur & Zur, 2011). Counselors who participate in social networking need to be educated not only on the technical dimensions of such a medium but also the ethical and legal complexities involved (Grohol, 2010; Younggren & Harris, 2010).

Accepting a client's friend request on a social networking site constitutes a dual relationship. The ethics of this dual relationship depend on the kind of information the client is privy to as well as the nature of the counselor–client online interaction (Zur & Walker, n.d.). Counselors who accept a client's friend request but allow the client to access only their professional profile, where the information shared is of a professional nature and available through other public sites, would not be creating an unethical dual relationship. However, should the counselor allow the client access to personal information or engage is posts that are of a personal nature, a boundary would be violated. Thus, the pivotal issue is not the counselor's participation on social media but rather the engagement at a personal level versus professional level with a client. "Counselors are prohibited from engaging in a personal virtual relationship with individuals with whom they have a current counseling relationship (e.g., through social and other media)" (ACA, 2014, Standard A.5.e).

In an attempt to provide guidance in managing these sensitive concerns, the ACA (2014) directs counselors to

1. employ separate professional and personal webpages and profiles (Standard H.6.a);
2. take precautions to avoid disclosing confidential information through public social media (Standard H.6.d); and
3. respect the privacy of the client's presence on social media, without consent to view such information (Standard H.6.c).

Email and Texting

Emails and texts might be ethical and practical when used for practice administration (e.g., scheduling appointments) or even as a vehicle for supporting a treatment plan or therapeutic homework (Bradley et al., 2011). As a form of communications, email and texting can be both efficient and effective. However, the use of these forms of communication as part of a counselor's professional practice can introduce a number of ethical challenges to the maintenance of professional boundaries.

A counselor who accepts and responds to a client's email/texts may foster an expectation that the counselor is available at all hours. Being "on call" clearly extends the boundaries of the professional relationship. Further, once the dynamic of responding to client emails at all hours and on all days has been established, failing to respond can be perceived as the counselor's disinterest or failure to care and thus shake the therapeutic alliance.

Counselors who choose to employ email and texting as part of their practice need to establish rules about the use of these modes of communicating and convey these rules during the process of gaining informed consent (Bradley et al., 2011). It is also important to help clients understand the risks and benefits of employing unsecured transmission technologies, including threats to the maintenance of confidentiality.

Applying an Ethical Decision-Making Model

While the boundaries defining a professional counseling relationship are essential to effective, ethical practice, the development and maintenance of these boundaries can at times be a challenge. There are times when a modification of the traditional boundaries defining counselor–client contact can be ethical and contribute to therapeutic effectiveness. However, it is also possible that variation from the more traditional boundaries of the counselor–client relationship can harm the therapeutic alliance and the client. It is crucial that decisions to deviate from a standard structure be done with a desire to protect and uphold the welfare and dignity of the client (Kitchener & Anderson, 2011).

The following case describes a condition that placed a counselor in an ethical dilemma regarding the boundaries guiding his interaction with a client. The case illustrates the use of an ethical decision-making model that invites the counselor to consider some critical questions and concerns. It is in responding to these questions that the counselor can navigate such a dilemma.

The Dilemma

Dr. Hansen is a licensed practicing counselor and has been in private practice for the past 11 years. In the past year, Dr. Hansen was elected to serve on the local school board.

The school board has committed to replacing all technological hardware and software across the entire system. Being new to the board, Dr. Hansen was initially unaware of this decision to proceed with a process that would require some vendors to come to the board and make formal proposals for their products and services. The contract to be awarded will be extensive and quite profitable for the vendor who is selected.

At his first board meeting, Dr. Hansen was able to review the list of vendors. In doing so, he was surprised to see that his client, Mr. R., was listed as one of the top three vendors being considered. The dilemma he is confronting is whether he should remain on the selection committee and participate in the selection or recuse himself from the process. Either decision appears to have a potential for harming the client and the counseling relationship.

In an attempt to resolve this dilemma, he engages in the following steps for ethical decision making, reflecting on the questions posed.

Identifying the Problem

What are the facts of the situation that appear to be contributing to the dilemma? Is the problem personal, clinical, legal, or ethical?

- Dr. Hansen is Mr. R.'s counselor. He is treating Mr. R. for job-related anxiety. Mr. R. has had difficulty closing deals recently and has been doubting his ability to succeed in this field.
- Dr. Hansen is a key member on the board and will be voting on a very lucrative contract for the winning vendor.

What is the nature of the problem (personal, clinical, legal, or ethical)?

- As a clinical problem, the board's decision could impact the therapeutic alliance created between Dr. Hansen and Mr. R. If by chance Mr. R. does not get the contract, it could shake his trust in Dr. Hansen and his belief in his competency. If he does get the contract, he may doubt that he did it on his own, without Dr. Hansen's influence.
- If Dr. Hansen recuses himself, that may stimulate questions that could threaten Mr. R.'s privacy and the confidentiality of their professional relationship.

Formulating the Ethical Concern

How might the dilemma relate to specific principles listed in the professional code of ethics?

- There has been a change in the relationship from professional to one of sales. The client should be allowed to refuse services related to the change (ACA, 2014, Standard A.6.d).
- While the decision will be that of the entire board, it appears that Dr. Hansen has extended the professional boundaries by possibly "purchasing" from his client (ACA, 2014, Standard A.6.b).
- Questions as to why Dr. Hansen would recuse himself may result in the client's privacy being threatened (ACA, 2014, Standard B.1.b).
- Given the situation, it appears that Dr. Hansen needs to consult with a colleague regarding the apparent dilemma (ACA, 2014, Standard C.2.e).

How might the dilemma relate to institutional policies (the school board)?

- The school board's regulations require that all members disclose any personal and/or professional relationships with potential vendors, service providers, and future employees.

How might the dilemma relate to Dr. Hansen's values, worldview, or personal needs?

- Other than concern for his client, there do not seem to be any personal needs being activated.

What is the nature and dimension of the dilemma?

- The dilemma seems to be primarily one of potential dual relationship and boundary crossing.
- It is hard to assess the potential for harm to the client and the counseling relationship, or the benefit that could be accrued concerning client welfare, regardless of the decision.

Generating Potential Courses of Action
What creative actions may address the needs of all parties and reflect ethical standards?

- Remain in the process and "pretend" that Dr. Hansen does not know the client.
- Share with the board that there is a possible conflict of a dual relationship.
- Recuse himself from the decision-making process.
- Consult with the client to discuss the cost and benefit of all options.

Consulting with a Colleague?
Is there value in consulting with a colleague to gain an alternative perspective?

- Dr. Hansen had time to consult with a colleague to see if there were other options or considerations that he may have been missing. No additional strategies were identified.

Assessing Each Option
What are the pros and cons for each possible course of action?

- Pretending as if he does not know the client is dishonest and would threaten the fidelity of their professional relationship.
- Sharing with the board—without the client's permission—would violate client privacy and confidentiality.
- Recusing himself might invite questions from the board members that could possibly violate confidentiality and client privacy.
- Unsure of the possible impact (both positive and negative) of each course of action on the client (physical, psychological, social realms), consulting with the client would provide some clarity.

Selecting a Course of Action
Given there is time before the vendor presentations begin, it would appear that the best decision is to discuss with the client the concerns about dual relationships and together discuss the pros and cons of each of the option. This would demonstrate respect for client autonomy, avoid harm by identifying possible costs to a decision, and demonstrate a desire to support client welfare.

- Options discussed were (a) to directly share the nature of the dual relationship and allow the board to decide if Dr. Hansen should continue to participate in the selection process and (b) to recuse himself from the decision-making process, providing a brief explanation of the concern about the dual relationship.
- Mr. R. was comfortable with Dr. Hansen explaining that they had a counselor–client relationship (without providing any further details) and recusing himself from the process. Mr. R. felt that recusal would remove any "hint" that he was getting any special consideration beyond the value of the proposal. Dr. Hansen suggested, and Mr. R. agreed, that he could tell the board that he had a professional relationship with one of the vendors (not identifying Mr. R. specifically), thus reducing the possibility of creating a bias among the members.

Implementing a Course of Action
Once the course of action has been selected, implement and assess the impact.

- The plan developed was for Dr. Hansen to share at the upcoming executive meeting of the board that he had a professional relationship with one of the vendors and therefore wished to recuse himself from the decision-making process.

Keystones

- Given the very intimate nature of the counseling relationship and the vulnerability of clients, the establishment and maintenance of rules defining the roles to be assumed and the behaviors that are appropriate (as well as inappropriate) is essential.
- Boundaries define the expected and accepted psychological and social distance between counselors and clients. Boundaries establish that space separating the client and their emotional needs from the counselor and their emotional needs.
- Boundary violations refer to the egregious and harmful transgressions of the counseling relationship that represent exploitation of the client's vulnerable position.
- A boundary violation occurs when a counselor misuses their power to exploit a client for the counselor's benefit. Boundary violations are always unethical and are likely to be illegal.
- Not all deviations from the traditional mode of operation constitute an ethical violation.

- Boundary crossings are brief, harmless, nonexploitative of the client, and not automatically viewed as unethical.
- Accepting a client's request to friend on a social networking site constitutes a dual relationship. The ethics of this dual relationship depend on the kind of information the client is privy to as well as the nature of the counselor–client online interaction.
- Counselors who choose to employ email and texting as part of their practice need to establish rules about the use of these modes of communicating and convey these rules during the process of gaining informed consent.

Additional Resources

Print-Based

Bradley, L., Hendricks, B., Lock, R., Whiting, P., & Parr, G. (2011). E-mail communication: Issues for mental health counselors. *Journal of Mental Health Counseling, 33*(1), 67–79.

British Psychological Society. (2012). *Supplementary guidance on the use of social media.*

Herlihy, B., & Corey, G. (2011). *Boundary issues in counseling: Multiple roles and responsibilities.* American Counseling Association.

Lopez, A. (2015). An investigation of the use of Internet-based resources in support of the therapeutic alliance. *Clinical Social Work Journal, 43*(2), 189–200.

Zur, O. (2007). *Boundaries in psychotherapy: Ethical and clinical explorations.* American Psychological Association.

Web-Based

Murdoch, J. W., & Connor-Greene, P. A. (2000). Enhancing therapeutic impact and therapeutic alliance through electronic mail homework assignments. *Journal of Psychotherapy Practice and Research, 9*(4), 232–237. http://www.ncbi.nlm.nih.gov/pmc/articles/PMC3330606/

Wade, M. E. (n.d.). Is it time to consider texting with clients? https://www.counseling.org/docs/default-source/ethics/ethics-columns/ethics_july_2015_texting.pdf?sfvrsn=1224522c_4

Zur, O., & Walker, A. (n.d.). To accept or not to accept? https://www.zurinstitute.com/socialnetworking.html

References

American Counseling Association. (2014). *ACA code of ethics.*

Balick, A. (2012). TMI in the transference LOL: Psychoanalytic reflections on Google, social networking, and "virtual impingement." *Psychoanalysis, Culture & Society, 17*(2), 120–136.

Borys, D. (1994). Maintaining therapeutic boundaries: The motive is therapeutic effectiveness, not defensive practice. *Ethics and Behavior, 4,* 267–274.

Bradley, L., Hendricks, B., Lock, R., Whiting, P., & Parr, G. (2011). E-mail communication: Issues for mental health counselors. *Journal of Mental Health Counseling, 33* (1), 67–79.

Everett, B. & Gallop, R. (2001). The link between childhood trauma and mental illness. Thousand Oaks, CA: SAGE.

Gottlieb, M. C., Younggren, J. N., & Murch, K. B. (2009). Boundary management for cognitive behavioral therapists. *Cognitive and Behavioral Practice, 16,* 164–171.

Grohol, J. (2010). Google and Facebook, therapists and client. *Psych Central.* http://psychcentral.com/blog/archives/2010/03/31/google-and-facebook-therapists-and-clients.

Gutheil, T. G., & Gabbard, G. (1993). The concept of boundaries in clinical practice: Theoretical and risk-management dimensions. *American Journal of Psychiatry, 150,* 188–196.

Kitchener, K. S., & Anderson, S. K. (2011). *Foundations of ethical practice, research, and teaching in psychology and counseling* (2nd ed.). Routledge/Taylor & Francis Group.

Lazarus, A. A., & Zur, O. (2002). *Dual relationships and psychotherapy.* Springer.

Smith, D., & Fitzpatrick, M. (1995). Patient–therapist boundary issues: An integrative review of theory and research. *Professional Psychology: Research and Practice, 26,* 499–506.

Sude, M. E. (2013). Text messaging and private practice: Ethical challenges and guidelines for developing personal best practices. *Journal of Mental Health Counseling, 35*(3), 211–227.

Younggren, J. N., & Harris, E. (2010, May/June). Risk management: Some additional thoughts on social networking. *National Psychologist,* 11.

Zilberstein, K. (2015). Technology, relationships, and culture: Clinical and theoretical implications. *Clinical Social Work Journal, 43*(2), 151–158.

Zur, O. (2001). Out-of-office experience: When crossing office boundaries and engaging in dual relationships are clinically beneficial and ethically sound. *Independent Practitioner, 21*(1), 96–100.

Zur, O. (2007). *Boundaries in psychotherapy: Ethical and clinical explorations.* American Psychological Association.

Zur, O. (2018). To cross or not to cross: Do boundaries in therapy protect or harm? *Psychotherapy Bulletin, 39*(3), 27–32.

Zur, O., & Walker, A. (n.d.). To accept or not to accept? Zur Institute. https://www.zurinstitute.com/socialnetworking.html

Zur, O. & Zur, A. (2011). The Facebook dilemma: To accept or not to accept? Responding to clients' "friend requests" on psychotherapists' social networking sites. *Independent Practitioner, 31*(1), 12–17.

Chapter 7

Counseling Beyond the Office Walls (Distance Counseling)

I can't believe it. I submitted 6 "skype" sessions for my client. They refuse to pay. I thought telehealth was accepted practice?

THE PRACTICE OF distance counseling has evolved from a hypothetical conversation to a professional reality. Counselors understand that the profession and professional practice is no longer limited to in-person, face-to-face interactions. It is safe to assume that future generations of counselors will interact with the world of distance counseling, by chance or design, in some form before their careers come to a close. However, counselors engaging in such practice will quickly come to realize that translating this understanding to actual practice introduces a number of practical, legal, and ethical challenges that extend beyond concerns regarding third-party payment. It is no surprise then that the most recent iteration of the ACA Code of Ethics (ACA, 2014) took great strides to more thoroughly address the realities of technology in counseling, with the inclusion of an entire section in the code, Section H. Distance Counseling, Technology, and Social Media. Perhaps the most telling statement came from the ACA's stipulation that not just distance counselors, but all counselors actively seek to increase their understanding of how technology continues to evolve our profession. Put another way, even the practitioner who hopes to avoid distance counseling altogether is still expected to have an understanding of its function and impact in our profession.

As suggested by our opening vignette, entry into the age of counseling and technology brings with it many challenges. Counselors are again left to navigate these new landscapes, armed with their wits and guided by the laws and ethical codes provided. After completing this chapter, readers will be able to

1. describe the various forms distance counseling may take,
2. identify the legal considerations and pitfalls associated with distance counseling,
3. identify the ethical considerations and pitfalls associated with distance counseling, and
4. apply existing ethical principles and codes in the context of distance counseling.

Distance Counseling on the Rise

It is safe to say that technology continues to have a meaningful impact on our daily lives. As technology evolves, so does the way we live. It is only natural that the advancement of technology has left its mark on the counseling profession and continues to do so every day. From an ethical perspective, core issues such as confidentiality and boundaries, for example, have become more complex as social media becomes a more culturally engrained means of communication and expression. This instance is one of many where operating ethically in the field has become more complex as technology-related realities have added to our list of considerations. Although a number of these scenarios will emerge in the coming chapters, this chapter is focused not so much on the impact of technology in counseling but instead on the legal and ethical considerations of using technology to provide counseling (i.e., distance counseling).

"Distance counseling," "cyber counseling," and "online counseling" are terms often used interchangeably to describe some sort of therapeutic process that is facilitated directly through the use of Internet-based technology. These can be both synchronous (e.g., video-, phone-, or text-facilitated counseling) or asynchronous (e.g., email-facilitated counseling). Why is distance counseling on the rise? You could easily say that developments in technology make such a rise inevitable. Whether termed cyber, online, or distance, this form of counseling is not without both its challenges and its benefits.

Distance counseling (the term we will use to refer to all forms of counseling facilitated directly through the use of Internet-based technology) provides a few unique advantages over its brick-and-mortar sibling. One of the most significant advantages comes from its accessibility. Many clients lack transportation and struggle to attend counseling physically. Others may have physical disabilities that make the process of attending counseling a difficult task (Remley & Herlihy, 2016). Consider also the rising number of clients seeking counseling due to social or anxiety-related issues. Distance counseling provides safe access to services for those who previously would have struggled to find it.

Distance counseling also comes with added conveniences of traditional counseling that many potential clients may find themselves drawn to. Depending on the format in which services are provided, scheduling may be more flexible. Flexibility also comes from a reduction in physical travel time that is often coupled with loss of work time. Beyond flexibility, distance counseling can also create a perceived sense of anonymity for clients, potentially decreasing anxiety and encouraging clients to ask for help and share (Bouchard et al., 2000; Haberstroh et al., 2007; Hamburger & Ben-Artzi, 2000; Heinlen et al., 2003; Lee, 2010; National Alliance on Mental Illness, 2014; Reeves, 2011; Rummell & Joyce, 2010; Sampson et al., 1997; Schultze, 2006; Shaw & Shaw, 2006; Wilson et al., 1997; as cited in Remley & Herlihy, 2016).

Despite a number of distinct benefits, the efficacy of technology-based counseling versus traditional therapy is still very much under debate. A whole chapter could be dedicated to that debate alone, but the purpose of this chapter is to unpack the legal and ethical realities of navigating the world of distance counseling. And, as will continue to be a theme throughout this text, not all of those realities are black and white.

Distance Counseling and the Law

Exploring uncharted waters comes with the inevitably of missteps. Such is the nature of the unknown. Much the same could be said for navigating the legal aspects of distance counseling. The law can often be incredibly complex; however, the biggest pitfall in terms of distance counseling is the lack of laws. Distance counseling is new professional territory, and there is little legal precedent to dictate best practices. Thus, providing distance counseling is an exercise in trying to avoid breaking the rules while the rules are still being written. Doing so is obviously easier said than done, and the question becomes, how best to tread such precarious ground? The ACA Code of Ethics provides some direction to its members by stating that counselors

> understand that they may be subject to laws and regulations of both the counselor's practicing location and the client's place of residence. Counselors ensure that their clients are aware of pertinent legal rights and limitations governing the practice of counseling across state lines or international boundaries. (ACA, 2014, H.1.b. Laws and Statutes)

While the direction is clear, the laws that guide its application are less so.

In the absence of legal precedent, counselors are well advised to stick closely to the ethical codes that guide them day to day. Although "legality" and "ethicality" are not synonymous, a counselor can best defend their actions when those actions align with what the average prudent professional would do. In most cases a line can be drawn from those actions directly to the ethical codes that dictate professional behavior. There are still a few legal hot spots that counselors should be aware of when providing distance counseling.

Interstate Practice

Distance counseling provides counselors with the opportunity to engage in professional practice across state lines. While expanding the scope of service, such interstate practice also invites the question of licensing. For example, the APA Practice Directorate reviewed data from 50 states and found that for most states, one needs to be licensed both in the counselor's own state and the state in which services are being delivered. This is but one area of concern for those whose use of distance counseling takes them beyond state boundaries. Since states vary in their regulation governing practice, it is essential for distance counselors to familiarize themselves with the laws of the land. Although state regulations are often similar, there can still be significant differences that are important to be aware of (e.g., scope of duty to warn). What makes the practice of distance counseling so complex is that the practice transcends geographic boundaries and thus blurs the line of what laws govern the process. The reality for practicing distance counselors is that they *may be* subject to the laws of multiple states at one time (ACA, 2014).

At the present time, there are more questions than answers. It is obvious, however, that the landscape of distance counseling is one to navigate with care.

Distance Counseling and Ethics

There is a bit more clarity on the ethical ins and outs of distance counseling than on the legal ones. The most recent iteration of the ACA Code of Ethics (ACA, 2014) includes standards that help guide the distance counseling professional in the delivery of digital services. The code also warns that counselors should "actively attempt to understand the evolving nature of the profession with regard to distance counseling" (ACA, 2014, p. 17). With that in mind, the section that follows addresses a selection of ethical issues and interpretations as they relate to distance counseling. It should be understood that this analysis is not exhaustive, and as the ethical code suggests, counselors are advised to continue to seek a deeper understanding of the ethical considerations at play as the field of distance counseling evolves. It is also worth noting that although the ACA Code of Ethics (ACA, 2014) is referenced here, various ethical codes exist that counselors may find themselves obliged to follow (e.g., AMHCA Code of Ethics, 2015). They would be well advised to consult each of those codes that apply.

Knowledge

As with all counseling, counselors are required to possess a certain level of knowledge and competency when providing services. Much is the same with distance counseling, but included with that is "technical" knowledge and skills in addition to ethical and legal considerations. The ACA (2014) has devoted an entire section (Section H) to issues of distance counseling, technology, and social media.

The ACA Code of Ethics directs its members to "develop knowledge and skills regarding related technical, ethical, and legal considerations (e.g., special certifications, additional course work)" (ACA, 2014, Standard H.1.a, p. 17). While the ethical mandate also suggests that special certifications or additional course work may be an option for obtaining this knowledge, it does not take a position that such training is necessary or required, only that one possess the knowledge and competency. The challenge is that the specific competencies required for such ethical practice are not identified and thus are left up to the practitioner to interpret and decide before practice.

Informed Consent and Security

The counselor's code of ethics provides direction for guiding counselors' decisions around issues of informed consent and maintenance of security while engaged in distance counseling (ACA, 2014, Standard H.2). As is true for all counseling contracts, acquisition of the client's informed consent remains a linchpin when engaging in distance counseling. However, the act of gaining such informed consent when engaged in distance counseling provides a number of unique challenges. In addition to common topics such as limitations in counseling or fees and billing information, the ACA Code of Ethics dictates that the following additional topics are to be addressed when providing distance counseling: physical location of practice, risk and benefits specific to distance counseling, technology failure and alternative methods of delivery, limits to confidentiality specific to a digital medium, anticipated response time, emergency procedures, time zone considerations, culture/language considerations, possible denial of insurance, and any existing social media policy (ACA, 2014, Standard H.2.a). It is worth mentioning that although the ACA Code of Ethics may at times provide only suggestions for certain practices, the language for this particular code is written so as to suggest that counselors are *required* to address the above considerations during informed consent.

From a security perspective, distance counseling also creates two particularly significant and unique considerations. The first is relatively straightforward in description but more complex in practice. Counselors are required to "take precautions to ensure the confidentiality of all information transmitted through the use of any medium" (ACA, 2014, Standard B.3.e, p. 7).

Even when providing traditional counseling, this is a reality most practitioners must navigate either when sending a client-related email or exchanging documents digitally. When this practice may become more complex is when the role of technology in the delivery of services is expanded by, for example, using real-time video to conduct sessions. What are the encryption standards of the associated websites? Are the video platforms compliant with industry standards of confidentiality? The answer to these and other related questions are not necessarily found in the ACA code as much as merely an indication that counselors are responsible for ensuring security. Once again, counselors are left to navigate the gray as they determine best practices. Case Illustration 7.1 highlights the complexity of this issue of encryption (see Case Illustration 7.1)

CASE ILLUSTRATION 7.1

SMILE, YOU'RE ON CAMERA

Arthur began seeing his counselor in the final year of his master's program. He presented with moderate to high levels of anxiety. During his intake, he indicated that he had also sought counseling toward the end of his undergrad program, as the upcoming life change/transition seemed to exacerbate the sense of worry and tension that he had become accustomed to.

Last month Arthur successfully completed his master's degree and was able to secure employment with a company on the West Coast. As was the case during his undergrad, this upcoming transition seemed to be worsening Arthur's anxiety, and so he and his counselor decided it would be best to continue weekly services via video counseling. Neither Arthur nor the counselor had engaged in distance counseling before, but having already established a working relationship, it seemed only logical to use the available technology to continue treatment. They ended up using a Google-based app to conduct the video sessions, since Arthur was already familiar with it and the counselor had heard from a colleague that Google-based products were HIPAA compliant.

FOR REFLECTION AND DISCUSSION

1. What are the potential ethical pitfalls in this case?
2. How might the counselor go about researching the legal and ethical aspects of this transition?

The second unique security consideration in distance counseling relates to client verification. This process in traditional counseling is straightforward: The client identifies themselves through the appropriate means (e.g., state-issued identification) at the onset of the counseling relationship, and the counselor verifies their identity thereafter each time the client walks through the door. In distance counseling, however, that process can become increasingly more complex, depending on the digital medium through which services are administered. Take, for example, a client to whom you provide counseling via real-time text/chat. When initiating the counseling relationship, the counselor can verify the client's identity through the same means as in traditional counseling. In what way, though, can they ensure that the person on the "other end" of the chat window each session is that same client? This difficulty of ensuring the identity of the individual as the client places the counselor at risk of breaching confidentiality. That is why, from an ethical perspective, distance counselors are required to take additional steps to verify their client's identity. This could take the form of code words, graphics, or other nondescript identifiers (ACA, 2014).

CASE ILLUSTRATION 7.2

THE MAN BEHIND THE CURTAIN

Selina had been providing real-time, chat-based counseling to Pam for approximately a year. Pam was referred to Selina by a family friend after a few months of struggling with a bout of depression. At the start of each session, Pam was asked to provide her birth date and address to confirm her identity. During one particular session, Selina observed some inconsistencies in Pam's behavior. According to Pam, she was feeling much better than she had in the previous week. She was unable to identify a specific reason for the turnaround but was adamant that she was a "new person." As she described all this, her messages were peppered with emojis and exclamation points, neither of which she had used in the past. Before the end of the session, Pam requested to cancel the next week's appointment. Feeling a bit uneasy, Selina asked Pam to confirm her identity again, this time by identifying her place of employment. Pam provided the info right away, and Selina ultimately canceled the following week's session.

FOR REFLECTION AND DISCUSSION
1. What procedural issues, if any, do you see in this exchange?
2. Did Selina sufficiently confirm the identity of her client?

The possibility of failing to establish the actual identity of the client when engaged in distance counseling presents another challenge at times when the counselor is legally required to warn a third party of potential danger from the client. Not only could the platforms employed during distance counseling restrict information normally gleaned via analyses of tone and nonverbals and thus make it difficult for counselors to assess a client's potential for violence or self- harm, but the platform employed might place the counselor in a position of not knowing the client's geographic location or even the client's real name.

Distance Counseling Relationship

Perhaps one of the most complex considerations in distance counseling from a clinical perspective is the nature of the distance relationship. When considering how significant the counseling relationship is on the therapeutic alliance, the issue of protecting and maintaining the relationship naturally becomes an issue of ethics. This issue is made more complicated when considered in the context of distance counseling. Perhaps the most obvious ethical issue/consideration relates back to the nature of electronic communication. Although the extent can vary based on the medium (e.g., video chat, real-time text chat), distance counseling can inherently rob the counselor of a variety of tools used to facilitate the process. Facial expressions or voice intonations are just two examples from a world of nonverbal and verbal cues that may be lost when providing distance services. Communication is obviously paramount to the therapeutic process, and without those tools, our ability to perform fundamental tasks such as modeling, assessing, or reflecting feelings can become much more difficult. The data gathered by visual and direct contact with a client is often invaluable. Exercise 7.1 invites you to consider what may be lost in your understanding of a client if non-verbal information was unavailable.

EXERCISE 7.1

MEANS OF EXPRESSION

Directions: For this exercise, imagine the quality of a day as falling on a scale of 1 to 10, with 1 indicating a very bad day and 10 a very good day. What would someone likely see if your day were a 10? a 5? a 1? Observations should be tangible and something that someone could see or hear.

Once you have completed your list of observations, exchange it with a partner.
1. Would you be able to make the same observations through a digital medium?
    a. If yes, would they look/sound different?
    b. If no, what observations could you make that would give you a similar amount of insight into how your partner is feeling on that day?

Another aspect of the counseling relationship that has been greatly impacted by technology, whether providing services traditionally or at a distance, is professional boundaries (see ACA, 2014, Standard H.4.b). Although the spirit of those boundaries remains the same, how they may manifest can be very different online. If, for example, a client was to run into their counselor at the local market, certain behaviors can be agreed on beforehand as to how each person can respond in a way that honors the wishes of the client while maintaining confidentiality. What if, however, the client and counselor are members of a community social media page or both active in an online political forum? Boundaries must still be maintained.

Applying an Ethical Decision-Making Model

The Dilemma

Barry, a licensed professional counselor, has been seeing his client Linda for approximately a year in his private practice in Delaware. Her presenting concerns have been related to moderate to severe social anxiety, which has seemed to decrease over the course of treatment. Due to an unexpected job opportunity, Linda shared last month that she would be relocating to Washington State. Barry has continued with sessions over the past month with increased focus on termination and assisting Linda to transition to a new counselor after moving. During her final session with Barry, Linda expressed concerns over transitioning to the new counselor she and Barry identified. "I just feel more comfortable with you since I've seen you for so long," Linda said. Linda asked if it would be possible, instead of starting with her new counselor the next week as planned, if she and Barry could continue with services digitally. Neither she nor Barry has any experience with distance counseling.

Identifying the Problem

What are the facts of the situation that appear to be contributing to the dilemma?

- Linda has an existing, face-to-face counseling relationship with Barry.
  - Linda is moving several states away and will be unable to attend counseling as she normally would.
- Linda and Barry created a tentative plan to terminate services over the course of a month and transition Linda to a new counselor in her new state.
- During their final session, Linda has requested to change the plan and continue services with Barry.

What is the nature of the problem (personal, clinical, legal, or ethical)?

- Personal
  - Linda would prefer to continue working with Barry despite relocating.
- Clinical
  - Linda has been attending counseling for approximately a year for anxiety-related issues. She does not pose a risk in terms of hurting herself our others. She is currently functioning at her baseline level with no impairment to her daily living and only moderate effects on her social life.
- Legal
  - Although licensed in Delaware, Barry is unaware of the licensure laws in Washington as related to base requirements or portability.

- Ethical
  - Barry is compelled to provide quality care in keeping with the ethical standards that guide his practices. The timing and nature of transitioning into a different delivery medium, however, may create ethical issues.

Formulating the Ethical Concern

How might the dilemma relate to specific principles listed in the professional code of ethics?

- Beneficence
  - Barry has a duty to promote Linda's well-being, and she *may* be better served by remaining with him for counseling since the relationship has been established.
- Fidelity
  - Barry committed to serving Linda upon taking her on as a client. The question is whether this commitment remains unchanged despite the upcoming changes in her life.
- Nonmaleficence
  - Barry must ensure that he causes no harm to Linda. Could terminating services with her cause harm?
- Knowledge and competency (ACA, 2014, Standard H.1.a)
  - Barry has no advanced training or experience with distance counseling. Having never provided such care, one can assume that Barry does not have the tools at his disposal to immediately engage a client digitally.
- Laws and statutes (ACA, 2014, Standard H.1.b)
  - Barry has no knowledge of the laws and regulations that may govern counseling in Washington State, whether traditional or distance.
    1. How might the dilemma relate to the counselor's values, worldview, or personal needs?

Generating Potential Courses of Action

What creative actions may address the needs of all parties and reflect ethical standards?

- Research online counseling over the next week and try to arrange to treat Linda digitally.
- Commit to working with Linda digitally but request a month to research the particulars.
- Process with Linda her hesitation and help ease her transition to the next counselor as much as possible.

Consulting With a Colleague?
Is there value in consulting with a colleague to gain an alternative perspective?

- Consult a colleague with knowledge of online counseling in terms of the specifics of providing distance care.
- Consult a colleague about possible consequences of each of the above options.

Assessing Each Option
What are the pros and cons for each possible course of action?

- Distance counseling is a specialized process. It has an impact on all elements of providing services, including responsibilities, consent, techniques and approaches, and so on. The chances of Barry learning within a short time all that is necessary to be considered competent at distance counseling are nearly nonexistent. There would also be little if no time to process with Linda the transition and how that would affect the therapeutic process.
- This option would provide Barry with more time, but there would either be a gap in services or Linda would transition from Barry to her new counselor and back to Barry within a very short span. Linda does not appear to be a danger to herself or others but transitioning to a new state will likely be a time of anxiety for her, and to be without support for a month could have adverse effects on her well-being. Yet if she did receive services and then attempt to just transition back to Barry, this could create a number of ripples in the therapeutic process that, again, could have a negative impact on her well-being.
- This option could allow Barry to support Linda to the best of his abilities and follow up if necessary after she transitions. He began the termination process appropriately and allowed for an adequate amount of time so as to meet his ethical obligations. She is also not in imminent danger from this change.

Selecting a Course of Action
After reviewing each option, select that which appears to be the best option available.

- The best option in this case is seemingly Option 3. Barry has provided quality care over the past year and allowed the termination process to play out appropriately and ethically. He has seen to connecting Linda with a new counselor, and there is no reason to believe that the impact of this transition will cause any more than an appropriate level of anxiety. Attempting to transition to distance counseling is likely to create a variety of ethical and potentially legal issues, many of which could have a significant negative impact on Linda's well-being, despite what her preferences may be.

Implementing a Course of Action
With option selected, implement and prepare to assess impact.

- Barry should process and normalize Linda's anxiety over this change but also highlight the positive aspects that come along with it (e.g., new job, new opportunity). He could consider arranging for a final, impromptu session prior to her move to give her plenty of time to convey her concerns and to prepare her for the transition.

Keystones

The impact of technology on the counseling profession is evident by the fact that the ACA Code of Ethics (ACA, 2014) took great strides to more thoroughly address the realities of technology in counseling, with the inclusion of an entire section in the code of ethics, Section H. Distance Counseling, Technology, and Social Media.

- "Distance counseling," "cyber counseling," and "online counseling" are terms often used interchangeably to describe some sort of therapeutic process that is facilitated directly through the use of Internet-based technology.
- A benefit often prescribed to distance counseling is that it provides greater accessibility to those who might otherwise be unable to participate in counseling.
- Distance counseling brings with it numerous ethical and legal challenges.
- The ACA Code of Ethics directs its members to "develop knowledge and skills regarding related technical, ethical, and legal considerations (e.g., special certifications, additional course work)" (ACA, 2014, Standard H.1.a, p. 17.
- The counselor's code of ethics provides direction for guiding counselors' decisions on issues of informed consent and maintenance of security while engaged in distance counseling (ACA, 2014, Standard H.2).
- A unique challenge for those engaged in distance counseling is that of client verification, especially when the counselor is legally required to warn a third party of potential danger from the client.

Additional Resources

Print-Based

Akister, J. (2003). Ethical and legal issues in e-mail therapy. *Journal of Family Therapy, 25,* 310.

Barak, A. (1999). Psychological applications on the Internet: A discipline on the threshold of a new millennium. *Applied and Preventative Psychology, 8,* 231–246.

Koocher, G. P., & Morray, E. (2000). Regulation of telepsychology: A survey of state attorneys general. *Professional Psychology: Research and Practice, 31,* 503–508.

Web-Based

Barnett, J. E. (2005). Online counseling: New entity, new challenges. *Counseling Psychologist, 33*(6), 872–880. https://doi.org/10.1177/0011000005279961

Mallen, M. J., Vogel, D. L., & Rochlen, A. B. (2005). The practical aspects of online counseling: Ethics, training, technology, and competency. *Counseling Psychologist, 33*(6), 776–818. https://doi.org/10.1177/0011000005278625

Tsan, J. Y., & Day, S. X. (2007). Personality and gender as predictors of online counseling use. *Journal of Technology in Human Services, 25*(3), 39–55. https://doi.org/10.1300/J017v25n03_03

Young, K. S. (2005). An empirical examination of client attitudes towards online counseling. *CyberPsychology & Behavior, 8*(2). http://doi.org/10.1089/cpb.2005.8.172

References

American Counseling Association. (2014). *ACA code of ethics*.

AMHCA Code of Ethics (2015). Retrieved from http://connections.amhca.org/HigherLogic/System/DownloadDocumentFile.ashx?DocumentFileKey=d4e10fcb-2f3c-c701-aa1d-5d0f53b8bc14

American Psychological Association Practice Organization. (2010). Telehealth: Legal basics for psychologists. *Good Practice, 41*, 2–7.

Bouchard, S., Payeur, R., Rivard, V., Allard, M., Paquin, B., & Renaud, P. (2000). Cognitive behavior therapy for panic disorder with agoraphobia in video-conference: Preliminary results. *Cyberpsychology & Behavior, 3*, 999–1007.

Haberstroh, S., Dufey, T., Evans, M., Bee, R., & Trepal, H. (2007). The experience of online counseling. *Journal of Mental Health Counseling, 29*, 269–282.

Hamburger, Y. A., & Ben-Artzi, E. (2000). The relationship between extraversion and neuroticism and the different uses of the Internet. *Computers in Human Behavior, 16*, 441–449.

Heinlen, K. T., Welfel, E. R., Richmond, E. N., & Rak, C. F. (2003). The scope of WebCounseling: A survey of services and compliance with NBCC standards for the ethical practice of WebCounseling. *Journal of Counseling & Development, 81*, 61–69.

Lee, S. (2010). Contemporary issues of ethical e-therapy. *Journal of Ethics in Mental Health, 5*, 1–5.

National Alliance on Mental Illness. (2014). *Technology is used to access mental health care and information*. http://www.nami.org

Reeves, A. (2011, September/October). Therapy and Skype. *Family Therapy Magazine*, 48–49.

Remley, T. P., Jr., & Herlihy, B. (2016). *Ethical, legal, and professional issues in counseling* (5th ed.). Pearson.

Rummel, C. M., & Joyce, N. R. (2010). "So wat do u want to wrk on 2day?": The ethical implications of online counseling. *Ethics & Behavior, 20*, 482–496.

Sampson, J. P., Jr., Kolodinsky, R. W., & Greeno, B. P. (1997). Counseling on the information highway: Future possibilities and potential problems. *Journal of Counseling & Development, 75*, 203–212.

Schultze, N. G. (2006). Success factors in Internet-based psychological counseling. *Cyberpsychology & Behavior, 9*, 623–626.

Shaw, H. E., & Shaw, S. F. (2006). Critical ethical issues in online counseling: Assessing current practices with an ethical intent checklist. *Journal of Counseling & Development, 84*, 41–53.

Wilson, F. R., Jencius, M., & Duncan, D. (1997). Introduction to the Internet: Opportunities and dilemmas. *Counseling and Human Development, 29*(6), 1–16.

Chapter 8

From One to Many

Couples and Families

Counseling is Counseling—I've worked with individual clients for more than ten years, moving into couple counseling is not a big deal.

THE COUNSELOR QUOTED above is not only misinformed but, if we assume, they begin to engage in marital and/or couples counseling without additional preparation, is behaving unethically and may be placing themself at risk for legal action. In the introduction of the text *The Essentials of Family Therapy*, Nichols (2009) asserts, "Family therapy isn't just a new set of techniques. It's a whole new approach to understanding human behavior" (p. 3).

At its foundation, couples and family counseling goes beyond working with one client to engaging with the clients' system, which includes not only each individual but also the way they function and influence one another (Nichols, 2009). Counselors engaged in couples and family counseling will need to formulate alliances not only with individual clients but also with the clients' system in order to effect changes in each of the members as well as their group dynamics. Engaging in couples and family counseling not only invites new theories and approaches but also introduces the counselor to a host of unique ethical issues and challenges (Knauss & Knauss, 2012; Lebow, 2014).

After completing this chapter, readers will be able to

1. explain the need to develop special competencies to engage as a couples and family counselor,
2. describe the possible challenges and ethical pitfalls of engaging in individual counseling while also working with that couple or family as a unit,
3. describe the unique considerations affecting the rules of confidentiality as well as the maintenance and release of records when working in couples and family counseling, and
4. identify the unit of treatment when working in couples and family counseling.

Special Competence: Not Simply Individual Counseling, Times Two

For some counselors, such as the one quoted in the introduction to the chapter, it seems to make sense that if they are trained in theories and techniques of counseling individuals, they should be able to engage with couples and families. Sadly, that is not only a misunderstanding but is something that positions them to act unethically.

As suggested by the standards set forth by the Council for Accreditation of Counseling & Related Educational Programs (2016), "students who are preparing to specialize as marriage, couple, and family counselors are expected to possess the knowledge and skills necessary to address a wide variety of issues in the context of relationships and families" (p. 31). It can be said the same is true for those in the field.

Counselors working with couples and families understand the truth to the statement that the whole is greater than the sum of its parts. Working with couples and families is not merely taking individual counseling times the number of members being seen. As noted in the International Association of Marriage and Family Counselors (IAMFC) Code of Ethics, "Couple and family counselors advocate for the family as a whole system while considering the uniqueness of each family member" (IAMFC, 2017, p. 1).

In couples and family counseling, the unit of treatment is not just the person, it is the set of relationships in which the person is embedded. Working with couples and families demands the knowledge and skill necessary to work with the entity of couple or family and the system dynamics that are active. Marriage and family counselors must balance a variety of therapeutic alliances not encountered when working with an individual client (Crane et al., 2010).

It is clear that training to work with individual clients does not adequately prepare one to navigate such a contextual and systemic dynamic, nor does it help one to address issues such as infidelity, abuse, and severe attachment disruption encountered in couples and family counseling (Shaw, 2001). Specialized training for those interested in working with couples and families is not only a good idea but also an ethical mandate. The need for specialized training is emphasized in the ACA Code of Ethics:

> Counselors practice in specialty areas new to them only after appropriate education, training, and supervised experience. While developing skills in new specialty areas, counselors take steps to ensure the competence of their work and protect others from possible harm. (ACA, 2014, Principle C.2.b., p. 8).

Counselors engaging in couples and family counseling need to develop competencies required for providing such specialty of service. In 2004 the American Association for Marriage and Family Therapy (AAMFT) adopted 128 specific competencies that represent the basic skills required of those engaged in marriage and family counseling (Nelson et al., 2007). Exercise 8.1 provides a sampling of the 128 competencies. Readers are invited to identify those competencies they currently possess and those for which further development is warranted. It is suggested that readers go to https://www.coamfte.org/Documents/COAMFTE/Accreditation%20Resources/MFT%20Core%20Competencies%20(December%202004).pdf in order to review all 128 competencies with the same intent of identifying targets for professional development.

EXERCISE 8.1

COMPETENCY FOR MARRIAGE AND FAMILY PRACTICE

Directions: Below is a table listing a sample of competencies suggested by the AAMFT as fundamental to effective, ethical practice. Review the list, identifying those for which you feel you have the competency and those which you feel should be targeted for your professional development, should you decide to engage in couples or family counseling.

Competency	Achieved	Target for Development
1.1.1 Understand systems concepts, theories, and techniques that are foundational to the practice of marriage and family therapy.		
2.1.1 Understand principles of human development; human sexuality; gender development; psychopathology; psychopharmacology; couple processes; and family development and processes (e.g., family, relational, and system dynamics).		
2.2.3 Develop hypotheses regarding relationship patterns, their bearing on the presenting problem, and the influence of extra-therapeutic factors on client systems.		
2.3.6 Assess family history and dynamics using a genogram or other assessment instruments.		
3.3.1 Develop, with client input, measurable outcomes, treatment goals, treatment plans, and aftercare plans with clients utilizing a systemic perspective.		
4.1.1 Comprehend a variety of individual and systemic therapeutic models and their application, including evidence-based therapies and culturally sensitive approaches.		

Competency	Achieved	Target for Development
5.3.2 Develop and assess policies, procedures, and forms for consistency with standards of practice to protect client confidentiality and to comply with relevant laws and regulations.		
6.1.2 Understand research and program evaluation methodologies, both quantitative and qualitative, relevant to marriage and family therapy and mental health services.		

Adapted from AAMFT, 2004.

Informed Consent

The right to informed consent reflects respect for individual freedom, autonomy, and dignity (Pope & Vasquez, 2016). It is fundamental to the ethics of therapy and counseling. The ACA Code of Ethics, for example, recognizes the valuing of a client's autonomy and directs its members

> to review in writing and verbally with clients the rights and responsibilities of both counselors and clients. Informed consent is an ongoing part of the counseling process, and counselors appropriately document discussions of informed consent throughout the counseling relationship. (ACA, 2014, Principle A.2.a, p. 4)

When applied in the context of couples and family counseling, the IAMFC, a division of the ACA, states quite clearly in Section B: "Confidentiality and Privacy" that

> each person who is legally competent and deemed an "adult" must be provided a confidentiality agreement with the couple and family counselor(s). The agreement must be time limited, consistent with legal statutes. The parameters of confidentiality must be agreed upon by the client and counselor. (IAMFC, 2017, p. 3)

A similar directive is found in the AAMFT Code of Ethics, where members are directed "to obtain appropriate informed consent to therapy or related procedures and use language that is reasonably understandable to the client" (AAMFT, 2015, Standard 1.2, p. 3). The specific types of information that need to be conveyed to clients in order for them to make an informed decision about engaging in counseling will vary as a reflection of the unique conditions of a counseling relationship. However, it is generally recognized that informed consent necessitates that the client: (a) has the capacity to consent; (b) has been adequately informed of significant information concerning treatment processes and procedures; (c) has been adequately informed of potential risks and benefits of treatments for which generally recognized standards do not yet exist; (d) has freely and without undue influence expressed consent; and (e) has provided consent that is appropriately documented. (AAMFT, 2015, Standard 1.2, p. 3)

While the elements depicted in the AAMFT Code of Ethics are very similar to those provided by the ACA for its members who are engaged in individual counseling, the application of these principles when employed with couples and families is often accompanied by challenges unique to that form of practice.

Given the reality that often those engaging in couples or family counseling fail to share the same level of interest or felt need opens the possibility that for some individuals, participation was less than entirely voluntary. Consider even the act of making a phone call to set up an initial appointment for couple or family counseling. A question could be asked as to the degree the caller is unduly coercing or influencing the other member(s) to participate in this appointment (Wilcoxon et al., 2007; Ramisch, 2010).

Another, somewhat unique challenge for those seeking to gain consent freely and without undue influence becomes evident when working with children engaged in family counseling. Even when those "children" are of legal age, the fact that their parents contracted for family counseling calls into question the degree to which the parents' social power invites coercion and thus a violation of the child's right to consent.

The issue of a child's consent or freedom to refuse engagement is complicated. While it is clear that some decisions are too complex for children to make independently and courts have historically supported parents' rights to engage children in therapy, even when against the child's wish (*Parham v. J.R.*, 1979), counselors must consider the ethical and "practical" need to gain a child's consent (or for those below legal age, assent) when engaging in family counseling. The IAMFC Code of Ethics states:

> Couple and family counselors should, prior to counseling of any minor client, obtain all court orders pertinent to that child's custody in order to assure they have obtained appropriate legal consents of treatment of their minor clients. Further, copies of the relevant court orders should be placed into the client's file along with their signed consents for treatment. (IAMFC, 2017, p. 3)

Boundaries and the Avoidance of Siding

When working with a couple, a counselor may find a reason to arrange for individual consultation even when contracted for relational work. While such individual sessions may prove useful when attempting to assess the potential for abuse or when assisting one member in developing a skillful way of presenting a sensitive issue, it also can introduce a myriad of difficulties.

Engaging with individual members of a couple or family, when working with such a collective, may unintentionally invite the sharing of "secrets" that in turn present a challenge to issues of confidentiality and privacy. Additionally, engaging in individual sessions can be invitations to the counselor to take sides, which moves the relationship from one of advocating for the couple or family to one advocating for a particular member. Under these conditions, the counselor will be crossing boundaries and creating a dual or multiple counselor–client relationships, having now begun to engage with a client in a way that is in addition to the initial treatment relationship (Cottone, 2005). Counselors working with couples and families need to remain neutral to avoid being triangulated into a dysfunctional family system (Stancombe & White, 2005). This is a point of ethical direction given by the AAMFT (2015): "Therapists, therefore, make every effort to avoid conditions and multiple relationships with clients that could impair professional judgment or increase the risk of exploitation" (Principle 1.3).

In addition to considering meeting with an individual family member as an extension of the couples and family counseling, there are situations in which the individual members of a couple or family may request engagement around personal (versus relational) issues. Engaging with an individual member outside of the relationship contract can create ethical challenges. Consider the challenge faced by the counselor working with a couple in marital counseling (see Case Illustration 8.1).

CASE ILLUSTRATION 8.1

THE SHIFTING OF THE PROFESSIONAL RELATIONSHIP

After attending couples counseling for over 3 months, the couple decides to amicably divorce. While the decision to divorce was the occasion to terminate the couples counseling, the counselor invited the couple to continue individually with her in order to cope with the stress often encountered during a divorce. Both the husband and wife agreed and began to see the counselor for their individual counseling.

What started amicably rapidly became contentious. Information shared in the individual sessions often placed the other spouse in a very negative light. Both the husband and the wife would share in their sessions information that argued for the "fault" of the divorce resting with the opposite party. Accusations of drug and alcohol abuse, infidelity, and even abuse were all presented as evidence for fault attributed to the opposite member of the relationship.

As legal action began to unfold, both parties requested the counselor's appearance in support of their position. Each of the client's personal lawyers requested copies of all records in hopes of finding support for their client's position. It was clear that shifting from the original couples counseling relationship to that of working individually with both the husband and wife not only moved the counselor into multiple roles but developed the expectations of advocacy for one or the other party.

FOR REFLECTION AND DISCUSSION

1. How might you respond to the opposing lawyers requesting your records?
2. What ethical concerns, if any, would you have had if the clients asked to continue with your counseling but as individuals?

Confidentiality: Sharing What, With Whom

All of the professional and legal standards that apply to confidentiality when engaged with counseling individuals also apply when working with couples and families. However, when working with couples and families, counselors face unique confidentiality concerns. Given the multiple members engaged in couples or marriage counseling, maintaining confidentiality can be a challenge. This is clearly noted in the IAMFC Code of Ethics, which states:

> Couple and family counselors must know and understand the limits of confidentiality, privacy, and privileged communication, including the fact that family members may disclose counseling-related information outside counseling thereby rendering the counselor no control over information thus shared. Therefore, couple and family counselors inform clients that in these instances, confidentiality, while desired, cannot be guaranteed. (IAMFC, 2017, p. 3)

Whereas most confidentiality concerns regarding individuals focus on the flow of information out of the counseling office for those working in multiple-client contexts, such as with couples and family counseling, special considerations also apply to disclosures within the couple or family context.

The AAMFT Code of Ethics highlights this unique challenge to confidentiality by stating, "In the context of couple, family or group treatment, the therapist may not reveal any individual's confidences to others in the client unit without the prior written permission of that individual" (AAMFT, 2015, Principle 2.2, p. 4).

A counselor can be tested along the lines of this principle when receiving "secret" information or private communication from one member of the couple or family. While the information may range from that of little concern to something quite significant, the process for handling such disclosures needs to be addressed.

When working with couples and families, it is essential to share the counselor's policy regarding such confidentiality and the maintenance of individual disclosures with all concerned at the outset of the counseling. This becomes especially important if the counselor will have individual meetings with the couple or family members or will accept phone calls or messages from any one member. The IAMFC Code of Ethics is clear on this point, stating, "Couple and family counselors do not participate in keeping secrets for or from clients" (IAMFC, 2017, p. 1).

Records Access

Record keeping, whether working with an individual, couple, or family, is an ethical responsibility that improves the quality of care and provides for continuity of treatment (ACA, 2015, Principle A.1.b; AAMFT, 2015, Principle 3.5). Given the unique nature of couples and family counseling, record keeping becomes somewhat of a challenge. If the counselor views the unit (i.e., couple or family) as the client, they may maintain a single, comingled record. Under these conditions, the ethical questions to be addressed include who has as access to the records and who controls the release of this information outside of the counseling relationship. The potential issues can be seen in Case Illustration 8.2.

CASE ILLUSTRATION 8.2

MY LAWYER NEEDS THE INFORMATION

The voice message was simple and clear. "Thank you for your help. I have decided to terminate counseling and file for divorce. Please send all of your case notes to my lawyer; you have his contact information. I want you to send all the notes covering the sessions we had as a couple as well as your notes on the individual sessions you had with my soon to be ex-wife. I am faxing my signed release of information form to your office."

FOR REFLECTION AND DISCUSSION

1. How would you respond to this request?
2. What steps might you have taken before fully engaging with the couple or even through your times together that may have mitigated the possibility of ethical or legal violations?

While the client's request in Case Illustration 8.2 was clear, a counselor unfamiliar with the AAMFT Code of Ethics may find the decision to disclose or to withhold unclear. The AAMT Code of Ethics directs its members to acquire

> written authorization ***from each individual*** [emphasis added], prior to providing access to or release of information. Marriage and family therapists provide clients with reasonable access to records concerning the clients. When providing a couple, family, or group treatment, the therapist does not provide access to records without written authorization from each individual competent to execute a waiver. Marriage and family therapists limit client's access to their records only in exceptional circumstances when they are concerned, based on compelling evidence, that such access could cause serious harm to the client. The client's request and the rationale for withholding some or all of the record should be documented in the client's file. Marriage and family therapists take steps to protect the confidentiality of other individuals identified in client records. (AAMFT, 2015, Principle 2.3, p. 4)

The IAMFC Code of Ethics directs its members to "provide only the records directly related to a particular individual, protecting confidential information related to any other client" (IAMFC, 2017, p. 3).

Clearly, when engaging in couples and family counseling, it is imperative that the counselor provide clients with a clear statement of policy regarding confidentiality, record keeping, and access at the time of acquiring consent to treatment.

Privileged Communications

Privileged communication is a legal extension of the ethical principle of confidentiality. When a patient or client has privilege, it is recognized that the information shared with a professional is protected from that professional's disclosure under the law.

Unlike confidentiality, which is held by the counselor, privilege belongs to the client. Only the client can take steps to assert or waive privilege. Placing the power with the client introduces some challenge for those working with couples and families. When considering the issue of privilege, counselors working with multiple participants need to be able to answer questions such as "Who is the client?" and "Who is the holder of the privilege?"

The identification of the holder of privilege when working as a marital counselor was central in a case in which a New Jersey psychologist refused to testify in court, claiming privilege. The situation was that the couple he was working with decided to seek a divorce. In the process, he was subpoenaed by the husband's lawyer to testify in court about information shared during conjoint therapy sessions. The wife refused to waive privilege, and as a result, the therapist refused to testify. The judge in this case ruled in favor of the wife's right to maintain confidentiality (Sugarman, 1974).

Similarly, in *Kinsella v. Kinsella* (1997), the Supreme Court of New Jersey determined that the communications made by one spouse in joint therapy sessions were protected from disclosure in a divorce action by the marriage and family therapist privilege. In both cases the couple was viewed as the client, with the couple holding privilege.

Regulations that define privileged communication and who within the helping professions can hold privilege sometimes vary state by state. For example, California law provides that where two or more persons are joint holders of the psychotherapist–patient privilege, a waiver of the right of a particular joint holder of the privilege to claim the privilege does not affect the right of another joint holder to claim the privilege (Leslie, 2012). This is contrasted to a ruling by a Virginia judge, who ruled that "when a husband and wife are in counseling sessions with a psychiatrist ... there is no confidentiality because statements were made not in private to a doctor, but in the presence of the spouse" (Herrington, 1979, p. 1).

Because of the possible variation in regulations across states, counselors working with couples and families need to familiarize themselves with the statutes and regulations governing privilege in their state of practice.

Applying an Ethical Decision-Making Model

When working with couples, a counselor will need to be aware of the nature of the therapeutic alliances being established, ensuring that alignment is with the couple rather than siding or aligning with any one member. While the directive is clear, its application can be challenging.

The following case describes a condition that placed a counselor in an ethical dilemma regarding therapeutic alliances, professional boundaries, confidentiality, and the process of gaining informed consent. The case illustrates the use of an ethical decision-making model that invites the counselor to consider a number of critical questions and concerns. It is in responding to these questions that the counselor can navigate such a dilemma.

The Dilemma

Dr. Fiora has been working with the Rigwalls for six sessions. The couple contracted for couples counseling when Mrs. Rigwall discovered that her husband was having an affair with a coworker. The couple agreed that they did not want this situation to destroy their marriage, and both were invested with Dr. Fiora not only to save but to improve their relationship.

During the initial session, Mr. Rigwall took full responsibility for the affair and, without making excuses, expressed his sorrow for violating his vows and hurting his wife. The couple understood that it would be difficult to move beyond this fracturing of the relationship but expressed a deep commitment to doing so. Throughout the sessions, the couple remained fully invested, disclosing their concerns and giving evidence of being willing to engage in the homework assignments provided by the therapist.

Given the progress that was being made, Dr. Fiora was entirely caught off guard when she received a voice message from Mr. Rigwall, stating: "Dr. Fiora, I need to see you privately. I do not want you to tell Sarah that I called. It is important and I trust you to keep it a secret. Please call me at the office—not the home—so that we can set up an appointment. I will come in anytime you are available, but please make it as soon as possible."

Not only did the phone call surprise Dr. Fiora, but the tone and content of the message aroused her concern for the client. While her immediate impulse was to call Mr. Rigwall, she was aware that such a response might jeopardize the trust and alliance that had been developed with the couple. Upon further reflection, she realized that she had not established rules regarding "private" information or confidentiality at the time of acquiring informed consent. She felt in a bind as to what was the ethical and responsible path to take. In an attempt to resolve this dilemma, she engaged in the following steps for ethical decision making, reflecting on the questions posed.

Identifying the Problem

What are the facts of the situation that appear to be contributing to the dilemma? Is the problem personal, clinical, legal, or ethical?

- Dr. Fiora is engaged in couples counseling, and one member of the couple is now requesting a private individual session.
- Dr. Fiora is aware that she failed to inform the couple about her policy regarding individual sessions and keeping secrets.

What is the nature of the problem (personal, clinical, legal, or ethical)?

- Clinically, she is concerned about the apparent crisis and urgency being expressed by Mr. Rigwall.
- Clinically, she is worried about the possibility of violating the trust of the couple and the therapeutic alliances she has created with the couple.
- Ethically, she is concerned about her failure to provide information about individual sessions, secret keeping, and sharing information that was called for during the acquisition of informed consent.
- She feels a concern for the client's welfare.

Formulating the Ethical Concern

How might the dilemma relate to specific principles listed in the professional code of ethics?

- The apparent need being expressed by the client requires a professional response, one addressing the client's dignity and promoting his welfare (ACA, 2014, Standard A.1.a).
- Clients have the right to understand all of the elements and conditions of the counseling so that they can make an informed decision about engagement (ACA, 2014, Standards A.2.a, A.2.b), especially as it relates to defining the couple as the client (ACA, 2014, Standard B.4.b).
- Engaging with multiple clients at the same time requires the counselor to inform them of the nature of the relationship the counselor will have with each, individually (ACA, 2014, Standard A.8).
- When engaged with clients, counselors need to support their right to privacy and respect for confidentiality (ACA, 2014, Standard B.1.c, B.1.d).

How might the dilemma relate to Dr. Fiora's values, worldview, or personal needs?

- In addition to a concern for her client, Dr. Fiora is struggling with what she now feels was her insufficient and perhaps unethical approach to gaining informed consent. She worries about possible legal ramifications.

What is the nature and dimension of the dilemma?

- The dilemma seems to be primarily one of potential dual relationship and boundary crossing that may violate the original therapeutic contract.
- Dr. Fiora is concerned about the potential harm to Mr. Rigwall, should she deny his request, while at the same time worrying about the harm that could be done to the therapeutic relationship with the couple if she acquiesces to the request.

Generating Potential Courses of Action

What creative actions may address the needs of all parties and reflect ethical standards?

- Simply ignore the message and not respond to the call, waiting until another request is made.
- Bring up the request in the next couple session with the hope of working the issue out in the context of their couples work.
- Gain agreement from both parties about the value of meeting individually and then schedule the meeting.
- Contact Mr. Rigwall and inform him of her concern for him as well as for the therapeutic relationship with the client, referring him to a colleague for individual sessions.

Consulting With a Colleague?

Is there value in consulting with a colleague to gain an alternative perspective?

- After sharing the situation with her colleague, the colleague offered another option for consideration. Perhaps she could see Mr. Rigwall with the goal of the session being to help him find a way to share his concern or issue within the context of the couples session.

Assessing Each Option

What are the pros and cons for each possible course of action?

- Ignoring the call reflects Dr. Fiora's need and not that of the client. It is abdicating her professional responsibility to treat her client with dignity and respect.
- Bringing up the phone call would be a violation of the client's right to privacy and could harm the level of trust between client and counselor.
- Inviting the couple to consider the value of individual sessions may stimulate a curiosity from Mrs. Rigwall as to why the suggestion is being raised and thus risk violation of Mr. Rigwall's privacy.
- Seeing Mr. Rigwall for one session with the goal of developing strategies for him to share the concerns in conjoint session might set the expectation of future continued individual meetings and position the counselor in the role of secret keeper if Mr. Rigwall refuses to share in joint session.

Selecting a Course of Action

Which course appears desirable?

- Given the concern for Mr. Rigwall, as well as the desire to maintain what had become a good working relationship with the couple, Dr. Fiora decided to return Mr. Rigwall's call. She was mindful of her need to control the discussion and the direction it took in order to limit Mr. Rigwall's disclosure while sharing her concern and recommendation for a therapist that he could see individually.

Implementing a Course of Action

Once the course of action has been selected, implement and assess the impact.

- Dr. Fiora called Mr. Rigwall and was able to control the direction of the conversation focusing on (a) her concern for his welfare; (b) highlighting her need to protect the trust in the relationship, given the progress made; and (c) providing him with three names of individuals whom she felt would be able to work with him, should he seek individual counseling.
- Mr. Rigwall expressed both his full understanding and his apology for what he defined as a moment of "panic." He asked if it would be appropriate to share that he had called and why at the next joint session.

Keystones

- At its foundation, couples and family counseling goes beyond working with one client to engaging with the clients' system, which includes not only each individual but also the way they function and influence one another.
- Working with couples and families demands the knowledge and skill necessary to work with the entity of couple or family and the system dynamics that are active.
- The need for specialized training is emphasized in the ACA Code of Ethics (ACA, 2014, Principle C.2.b).
- Engaging with individual members of a couple or family, when working with such a collective, may unintentionally cross boundaries and invite the sharing of secrets and thus presenting a possible conflict with confidentiality and privacy.
- According to the AAMFT, a therapist cannot disclose individual confidence without prior written permission to do so (AAMFT, 2015, Principle 2.2).
- The AAMFT Code of Ethics directs counselors, when sharing records, to acquire "written authorization **from each individual** [emphasis added], prior to providing access or release of information" (AAMFT, 2015, Principle 2.3).
- Establishing rules regarding issues such as record keeping and access, confidentiality, and private/individual sessions needs to be part of the informed consent process when working with couples and families.

Additional Resources

Print-Based

Caldwell, B. E. (2015). *User's guide to the 2015 AAMFT code of ethics.* American Association for Marriage and Family Therapy.

Gehart, D. R. (2018). *Mastering competencies in family therapy: A practical approach to theory and clinical case documentation* (3rd ed.). Cengage.

International Association of Marriage and Family Counselors. (2017). *IAMFC code of ethics.*

Volini, L. A. (2018). *The national licensing exam for marriage and family therapy: An independent study guide* (2nd ed.). MFT Licensing Exam LLC.

Wilcoxon, S. A., Remley, T. P., & Gladding, S. T. (2013). *Ethical, legal, and professional issues in the practice of marriage and family therapy* (5th ed.). Pearson.

Web-Based

American Association for Marriage and Family Therapy. (2015). Code of ethics. https://www.aamft.org/Legal_Ethics/Code_of_Ethics.aspx

Koocher, G. P., & Keith-Spiegel, P. (2016). Caught in the middle: Ethical challenges in working with couples and families. http://www.continuingedcourses.net/active/courses/course085.php

Shaw, E. (2011). Ethics and the practice of couple and family therapy. https://www.psychology.org.au/publications/inpsych/2011/feb/shaw

References

American Association for Marriage and Family Therapy Code of Ethics (2015). Retrieved from: https://www.aamft.org/Legal_Ethics/Code_of_Ethics.aspx

American Association for Marriage and Family Therapy. (2004). Marriage and family therapy core competencies. https://www.coamfte.org/Documents/COAMFTE/Accreditation%20Resources/MFT%20Core%20Competencies%20(December%202004).pdf

American Association for Marriage and Family Therapy. (2018). Code of ethics. https://www.nvc.vt.edu/mft/files/guides/Attachment%20D_Code%20of%20Ethics.pdf

American Counseling Association. (2014). *ACA code of ethics.*

Council for Accreditation of Counseling and Related Educational Programs (CACREP) (2016). Retrieved from: https://www.cacrep.org/for-programs/2016-cacrep-standards/

Cottone, R. R. (2005). Detrimental therapist–client relationships—beyond thinking of "dual" or "multiple" roles: Reflections on the 2001 AAMFT code of ethics. *American Journal of Family Therapy, 33*(1), 1–17.

Crane, D. R., Shaw, A. L., Christenson, J. D., Larson, J. H., Harper, J. M., & Feinauer, L. L. (2010). Comparison of the family therapy educational and experience requirements for licensure or certification in six mental health disciplines. *American Journal of Family Therapy, 38,* 357–373.

Dishion, T. J., & Stormshak, E. A. (2007). Ethical and professional standards in child and family interventions. In T. J. Dishion & E. A. Stormshak (Eds.), *Intervening in children's lives: An ecological, family-centered approach to mental health care* (pp. 241–264). American Psychological Association.

Herrington. B. S. (1979). Privilege denied in joint therapy. *Psychiatric News, 14*(9), 1–9.

International Association of Marriage and Family Counselors. (2017). *IAMFC code of ethics.*

Kinsella v. Kinsella, 150 N.J. 276 (1997).

Knauss, L. K. & Knauss, J. W. (2012). Ethical issues in multiperson therapy. In S. J. Knapp, M. C. Gottlieb, M. M. Handelsman, & L. D. VandeCreek, (Eds.), *APA handbook of ethics in psychology, vol 2: Practice, teaching, and research* (pp. 29–43). American Psychological Association. https://doi.org/10.1037/13272-003

Lebow, J. (2014). Ethics and values. In J. Lebow (Ed.), *Couple and family therapy: An integrative map of the territory* (pp. 207–219). American Psychological Association.

Leslie, R. (2012). *Joint holders of the privilege—meaning and implications.* https://www.cphins.com/joint-holders-of-the-privilege-meaning-and-implications/

Nelson, T. S., Chenail, R. J., Alexander, J. F., Crane, D. R., Johnson, S. M., & Schwallie, L. (2007). The development of core competencies for the practice of marriage and family therapy. *Journal of Marital and Family Therapy, 33*(4), 417–438.

Nichols, M. P. (2009). *The essentials of family therapy* (4th ed.). Pearson.

Parham v. J.R., 442 U.S. 584 (1979).

Pope, K. S., & Vasquez, M. J. T. (2016). *Ethics in psychotherapy & counseling: A practical guide* (5th ed.). Wiley.

Ramisch, J. (2010). Ethical issues in clinical practice. In L. Hecker, (Ed.), *Ethics and professional issues in couple and family therapy.* Routledge.

Shaw, E. (2001, May). The Anxiety in Maintaining the Couple Relationship. *Psychotherapy in Australia.*

Stancombe, J., & White, S. (2005). Cause and responsibility: Towards an interactional understanding of blaming and "neutrality" in family therapy. *Journal of Family Therapy, 27,* 330–351.

Sugarman, D. A. (1974). Diary of a subpoenaed psychologist. *New Jersey Psychologist, 24*(3), 13–18.

Wilcoxon, A. A., Remley, T. P., Gladding, S. T., & Huber, C. H. (2007). *Ethical, legal and professional issues in the practice of marriage and family therapy* (4th ed.). Pearson.

Chapter 9

Evidence-Based Treatment and Practice

I just try lots of different things that feel right and then see what works.

THE COUNSELOR QUOTED in the introduction to this chapter was responding to a question about his approach to treatment planning. It would appear that his planning is little if any, and the selection of interventions may be somewhat happenstance. This approach is not a reflection of good professional practice or an ethical practitioner.

In their efforts to assist their clients, counselors are directed by the ACA Code of Ethics to work with their clients "jointly in devising counseling plans that offer reasonable promise of success and are consistent with the abilities, temperament, developmental level, and circumstances of clients" (ACA, 2014, Principle A.1.c., p. 4). To this end, counselors have been trained in the theory and research that support professional practice, and they take great pains in the establishment of their case conceptualization and treatment plans.

The current chapter reviews the concept and nature of evidence-based practice as a foundation for ethical treatment planning and professional practice. After completing this chapter, readers will be able to

1. describe what is meant by the terms "evidence-based practice," "evidence-based treatment," and "practice-based treatments";
2. provide an ethical basis for employment of evidence-based practice and evidence-based treatments; and
3. explain what is meant by a "two-stage" process of developing professional competency.

Evidence-Based Practice

Evidence-based practice (EBP) has been defined as "the integration of the best available research with clinical expertise in the context of patient characteristics, culture, and preferences" (APA Presidential Task Force on Evidence-Based Practice, 2006, p. 273). EBP includes practices that are informed by research, in which "the characteristics and consequences of environmental variables are empirically established, and the relationship directly informs what a practitioner can do to produce a desired outcome" (Dunst et al., 2002, p. 3). EBP is intended to comprise the thoughtful integration of best available evidence with clinical expertise and client values (Sackett et al., 2000).

Two of the main goals behind EBP are to increase the quality of treatment and to increase accountability. The goal is to provide clients with those interventions that have been supported as effective (Spring, 2007) and meet the ethical mandate of the ACA Code of Ethics to engage techniques "*that offer reasonable promise of success*" (ACA, 2014, Principle A.1.c, p. 4).

Counselors engaged in EBP make practice decisions guided by (a) current research on effective treatment for a particular problem or disorder and (b) research and clinical expertise on what works for a particular client. Counselors employing an evidence-based approach to their practice will identify the client's problem and goals, review the best available research relevant to those issues and goals, and then collaboratively develop a treatment plan with the client (Drisko, 2017). Such a process is delineated in Case Illustration 9.1.

CASE ILLUSTRATION 9.1

A DOG LOVER'S NIGHTMARE

The 32-year-old client not only loved animals—especially dogs—but had crafted a very successful business as an animal walker and caretaker. Her world came crashing down after one of the dogs, with whom she had a positive relationship, attacked her, which resulted in her hospitalization for over 20 puncture wounds. It was later discovered that the dog was suffering from a brain lesion that accounted for the sudden turn to aggressive behavior, but that information did not reduce the PTSD currently engulfing the client's life.

The client engaged in counseling with a counselor who employed a psychodynamic orientation. Frustrated with the lack of progress and the emotional distress that seemed to be getting worse, she sought a referral to a counselor who specialized in anxiety disorders. This second counselor employed a process of thoroughly assessing the client's symptoms and narrative. The information gathered was employed to inform the client about techniques that have support for their effectiveness. The counselor was familiar with various outcome studies showing the effectiveness of cognitive processing therapy and eye movement desensitization and reprocessing therapy. Following a discussion with the client, exposure-based intervention, one employing a systematic presentation of fear stimuli, was selected as the planned intervention. The counselor and client agreed that this approach not only would provide a process that has demonstrated effectiveness but was one that fit the client's lifestyle and values.

FOR REFLECTION AND DISCUSSION

1. What, if any, responsibility does the first counselor have to provide the new counselor with their clinical insights or notes?
2. How would you have responded to the client's notification of her desire to go to another counselor?

Implementation of EBP has been increasingly required across a variety of counseling settings, such as in schools (Carey & Dimmitt, 2008; Dimmitt et al., 2007; Forman et al., 2013) and nonprofit human services organizations (McLaughlin et al., 2010). Thus, for those working in these contexts, EBP is a must. However, the employment of empirically based practice is more than a practical response to organizational mandates; it also represents adherence to a call for ethical practice. The ACA Code of Ethics states, *"Counselors have a responsibility to the public to engage in counseling practices that are based on rigorous research methodologies"* (ACA, 2014, p. 8).

Treatment Selection

For counselors to truly engage in EBP, they must anchor treatment in the best scientific evidence available and use the techniques and psychological approaches that have scientific support. Evidence-based treatments, also called empirically supported treatments, have been described as clearly delineated (often manualized) interventions that have produced a therapeutic change in controlled trials (Kazdin, 2008). These are treatments that have been shown to improve client outcomes in more than one randomized clinical trial (Chambless & Ollendick, 2001). Employment of detailed, even manualized, interventions does not preclude the counselor's use of their clinical expertise to apply these treatments in a manner that addresses their clients' unique characteristics, cultures, and preferences (APA Presidential Task Force on Evidence-Based Practice, 2006).

Efforts put forth by the ACA (Morkides, 2009) and the American Counseling Association Practice Research Network (Bradley et al., 2005) have revealed that evidence-based interventions are critical to the optimal functioning of counselors. It has been suggested that counselors who do not employ research and empirical findings to inform diagnosis, assessment, and treatment decisions may be doing their clients a disservice (Shimokawa et al., 2010).

Beyond the issue of potential disservice, counselors who rely exclusively on their intuition or personal experience as the basis for the formulation of treatment plans also may be violating the ethical directive provided by the ACA that calls for counselors to *"use techniques/procedures/modalities that are grounded in theory and/or have an empirical or scientific foundation"* (ACA, 2014, Principle C.7.a, p. 10).

Exercise 9.1 invites you to interview practitioners regarding their knowledge, use, and experience with empirically supported interventions.

Practitioners sensitive to the need to incorporate research findings into their practice decisions need to remain up-to-date on the research surrounding the effectiveness of various interventions. The Society of Clinical Psychology, Division 12 of the APA, provides an alphabetized list of psychological treatments, including a description of the intervention, research support, clinical resources, and training opportunities. Table 9.1 provides an abbreviated listing of a number of these treatments. Those interested in a full listing, along with case studies, should consult the society's webpage (https://www.div12.org/treatments/).

EXERCISE 9.1

EMPIRICALLY SUPPORTED INTERVENTIONS: PERSPECTIVE FROM THE FIELD

Directions: The employment of an intervention within the context of a controlled study will be different from the application of that intervention to any one person being treated in individual practice. The current exercise invites you to interview practitioners who are familiar with the concept of empirically supported interventions. You may find it valuable to share your findings with a colleague or classmate.

1. When developing your treatment plans, do you consider research supporting particular forms of intervention?
2. Have you received specific training in the utilization of any empirically supported interventions? If so, which interventions? If not, what are your feelings about the employment of these strategies?
3. If you have employed empirically supported interventions in your practice, have you found any specific need to modify the protocol? If so, what was the reason for this modification?
4. When employing an intervention, how do you monitor effectiveness in terms of progress and outcome?

TABLE 9.1. PSYCHOLOGICAL TREATMENTS

The following represents an abbreviated list of treatments identified by the Society of Clinical Psychology, Division 12 of the APA. Details and ratings of the degree to which the evidence supports treatment effectiveness can be viewed https://www.div12.org/treatments/.

- Acceptance and Commitment Therapy for Obsessive-Compulsive Disorder
- Behavioral and Cognitive Behavioral Therapy for Chronic Low Back Pain
- Biofeedback-Based Treatments for Insomnia
- Cognitive Adaptation Training (CAT) for Schizophrenia
- Cognitive and Behavioral Therapies for Generalized Anxiety Disorder
- Cognitive Behavioral Analysis System of Psychotherapy for Depression
- Cognitive Behavioral Therapy for Obsessive-Compulsive Disorder
- Cognitive Behavioral Therapy for Panic Disorder
- Dialectical Behavior Therapy for Borderline Personality Disorder
- Eye Movement Desensitization and Reprocessing for Post-Traumatic Stress Disorder
- Family Psychoeducation for Schizophrenia
- Interpersonal and Social Rhythm Therapy (IPSRT) for Bipolar Disorder
- Motivational Interviewing, Motivational Enhancement Therapy (MET), and MET plus CBT for Mixed Substance Abuse/Dependence
- Prolonged Exposure Therapy for Post-Traumatic Stress Disorder
- Psychoanalytic Treatment for Panic Disorder
- Self-System Therapy for Depression
- Short-Term Psychodynamic Therapy for Depression
- Stress Inoculation Training for Post-Traumatic Stress Disorder
- Transference-Focused Therapy for Borderline Personality Disorder

TABLE 9.2. CRITERIA FOR IDENTIFYING EVIDENCE-BASED TREATMENT

1. Has the research used **randomized clinical trials** demonstrating effectiveness?
2. Has the research **demonstrated effectiveness of the intervention** using different samples and varied settings?
3. Are outcome, dependent variables, and treatment interventions **clearly defined?**
4. Has the intervention been administered according to procedures and standards that can be used by others? **Feasibility** of the practice or intervention.
5. **Assurances of fidelity**—have interventions been implemented according to standard ethical practices, and are the procedures transparent?
6. Is the intervention **theoretically grounded**?
7. Have the practices or interventions been used with **diverse populations**?

Adapted from Smith, 2011, pp. 3-4.

While there are clear limitations to current research, and ongoing evaluation of intervention strategies continues, counselors interested in using protocols and treatments that reach the threshold of being evidence-based would do well to review the criteria suggested for the assessments found in Table 9.1. Table 9.2 lists an adaptation of the seven criteria suggested by Smith (2011) for determining whether a protocol or treatment has reached the threshold of being evidenced based.

Issue of Competence

Counseling research continues to provide new insights into the human condition as well as techniques and strategies that can be brought to bear in the facilitation of our clients' achievement of their desired goals. Counselors responsive to the call for the implementation of EBP will need to develop and refine existing clinical skills, expand knowledge and awareness of emerging research, and perhaps at times reconcile philosophical differences between EBP and their respective disciplines (Tarvydas et al., 2010).

While it may seem to be obvious, the ACA makes it explicitly clear that "counselors practice only within the boundaries of their competence, based on their education, training, supervised experience, state and national professional credentials, and appropriate professional experience" (ACA, 2014, Principle C.2.a, p. 8.).

Given the unfolding science of our profession, the effort to maintain and improve clinical competence is intrinsic to ethical practice for counselors (Jennings et al., 2005). Counselors are ethically responsible to "maintain their competence in the skills they use, are open to new procedures, and remain informed regarding best practices for working with diverse populations" (ACA, 2014, Principle C.2.f, p. 9).

For those in the field concerned about maintaining professional competency and developing competencies in new, emerging interventions, participation in professional development is essential. While workshops, distance learning, and e-learning formats are most often used to develop knowledge about new strategies and techniques in counseling, knowledge alone is insufficient for ethical practice. The ACA provides online courses, webinars, podcasts, and reading materials aimed at supporting a counselor's professional development (see web-based resources at the end of this chapter).

Practicing within the boundaries of one's competence means that a counselor has both the knowledge of the treatment in use and the ability to implement it at an acceptable standard (Fairburn & Cooper, 2011). Therefore, maintaining one's competency requires a two-stage approach to professional development (Beidas & Kendall, 2010; Weissman et al., 2006). A two-stage approach starts with a didactic presentation of the treatment along with a demonstration. The goal of the second stage is the translation of this knowledge into practice, which requires that the counselor perform under the supervision of one who is proficient in the treatment method.

The need for both education and supervision is identified in the ACA Code of Ethics, which states that counselors engage in a new specialty area or employ a new technique "only after appropriate education, training and supervised experience" (ACA, 2014, Principle C.2.b, p. 8).

When Scientific Foundation Is Unavailable

While there are numerous issues, both professional and conceptual, surrounding the issue of empirically supported treatments, the discussion serves to highlight the need for ethical counselors to engage in practice with forethought and when possible to engage theory and research to guide practice decisions. A question emerges as to what a counselor should do when there is no empirically supported intervention for the issue being presented. What is the ethical counselor to do when empirical support is lacking or unclear regarding best practice for any one specific case?

One suggestion proffered is for counselors to move from an evidence-based approach to a "practice-based" evidence approach (Margison et al., 2000). The focus remains the same in that both approaches seek to deliver services that provide the client with the best chance of achieving the desired outcome. The counselor employing a practice-based evidence model of service will systematically collect "information on the process of change and outcome" (Green & Latchford, 2012, p. 87). Case Illustration 9.2 provides an example of one counselor's use of an experimental model to monitor their practice effectiveness.

Counseling practitioners who evaluate their local interventions can use the findings to improve their practice and to be accountable to their stakeholders (Baker, 2012). Thus, a practice-based evidence model reflects the ethical mandate for counselors to monitor their effectiveness. "Counselors continually monitor their effectiveness as professionals and take steps to improve when necessary. Counselors take reasonable steps to seek peer supervision to evaluate their efficacy as counselors" (ACA, 2014, Principle C.2.d, p .8).

CASE ILLUSTRATION 9.2

APPLYING EXPERIMENTAL DESIGN IN PRACTICE

The following is one counselor's reflection on the value of systematic data collection as a tool for guiding practice decisions.

"Well, I have always been interested in the science underlying our profession. However, once I got into my private practice, I realized that the setting and the needs of the clients did not support a 'rigid-experimental' paradigm. However, I have seen a number of clients whose presenting concerns allowed for the application of an AB single-subject design to intervention assessment. It would not pass the criteria for a research article, but in one case, for example, gathering baseline data helped motivate the client to employ the mindfulness intervention discussed in the session. The client, a computer programmer, was having trouble at work, noting that he had become quite distracted and was making numerous programming errors. He believed that he may need medication and that perhaps he was exhibiting a form of adult-attention deficit. The data he shared at intake suggested that the issue might be a response to the increased stress and pressure experienced at work and that his 'distractions' were attempts at stress reduction. I invited him to gather data on the number of corrections he would need to make over the course of the upcoming week as well as make brief notes about the work he was doing at the time and any other things that were happening in the office at the moments of his distraction. In reviewing these data, we discovered that he averaged about 5 corrections a day and that quite often these were associated with a text or question coming from a colleague. The client noted that these 'interruptions' just seemed to add to his stress and concern about getting his work done, and as a result, he would find himself drifting off and fantasizing about his upcoming vacation. We processed the information and decided to 'try' to incorporate breaks (mini-vacations) in his work as a way of renewing his energy and ability to focus.

The client was instructed in a mindfulness technique that focused on breathing. I had him close his eyes and engage in slow, rhythmic breathing. I asked him to focus on the cold air as it came through his nose and the warmer air as it left his body through his mouth. Initially, he resisted, saying that he was already taking too much time on projects and this would take more time. We reviewed the data and found that his periods of distraction often lasted up to 5 minutes in duration. I suggested that we could download a meditational chime on his computer, one that would signal every 90 minutes as a cue to engage in his breathing and would signal after 1 minute to stop and return his focus to work. While skeptical, he felt that the 1-minute reminder would at least be a step in the right direction. He continued the daily monitoring of his errors and corrections and plotted these data.

He was excited to see that his time off task had been reduced, as had his frequency of error. This simple process of gathering data not only supported the value of the intervention but increased the client's interest and motivation to continue to engage in counseling."

FOR REFLECTION AND DISCUSSION

1. Do you see any potential "costs" to the counseling relationship or the therapeutic dynamic with the counselor focusing on the gathering of objective data?
2. Would it be ethically responsible for the counselor to publish these case findings?

Applying an Ethical Decision-Making Model

It is clear that ethical practice requires that counselors "*engage in counseling practices that are based on rigorous research methodologies*" (ACA, 2014, p. 8). Further, the ethical counselor is directed to employ "*techniques/procedures/modalities that are grounded in theory and/or have an empirical or scientific foundation*" (ACA, 2014, Principle C.7.a, p. 8). While the directive is clear, its application not always that simple.

The Dilemma

Dr. Hansen, a licensed professional counselor, has been in practice for over 15 years. His practice is primarily with adults experiencing anxiety and depression. He describes his theoretical orientation as humanistic and existential and his preferred mode of counseling as "nondirective."

He recently engaged with a new client, Ms. K., an attractive, bright woman who presented to counseling because of her frustration with a long-standing history of failed relationships. Her description highlighted what appeared to be her difficulty in making good relational choices. "I seem to get hooked up with the biggest losers on earth! It is just that I am afraid I'm going to be alone the rest of my life—so I guess I get in positions where I would rather take anyone, as opposed to having no one."

As her story unfolded, it became clear to Dr. Hansen that he was engaging with a person manifesting a borderline personality disorder. While appreciating the need and value of building a therapeutic relationship high in trust and rapport, something that he felt quite competent in doing, he was concerned that his nondirective approach might not be as effective in working with such a client and that perhaps referral was in her best interest.

Identifying the Problem

- What are the facts of the situation that appear to be contributing to the dilemma? Is the problem personal, clinical, legal, or ethical?
  - Dr. Hansen has diagnosed the client as manifesting a borderline personality disorder.
  - Dr. Hansen's theoretical model is humanistic and nondirective.
  - While understanding the need and value for the development of a trusting therapeutic relationship, Dr. Hansen questions the efficacy of a nondirective approach to treatment.
- What is the nature of the problem (personal, clinical, legal, or ethical)?
  - Clinically, Dr. Hansen questions his competency to provide the most effective service to the client.
  - Clinically, he is concerned that any suggestion of needing to refer might be interrupted by the client as "abandonment."
  - Ethically, he understands the literature on the efficacy of dialectical behavioral therapy with such a client. His concern is that even though he has read quite a bit about the approach, he has never used it under direction or supervision.

Formulating the Ethical Concern
- How might the dilemma relate to specific principles listed in the professional code of ethics?
  ○ Counselors are directed to "*engage in counseling practices that are based on rigorous research methodologies*" (ACA, 2014, p. 8).
  ○ Counselors practice in specialty areas new to them only after appropriate education, training, and supervised experience (ACA, 2014, *Principle* C.2.b).
  ○ When lacking competence to provide service, "*counselors are knowledgeable about culturally and clinically appropriate referral resources*" (ACA, 2014, *Principle* A.11.a, p. 6).
- How might the dilemma relate to Dr. Hansen's values, worldview, or personal needs?
  ○ Dr. Hansen is concerned for the well-being of the client and, while philosophically wedded to a humanistic theoretical orientation, understands the research that supports a directive dialectical behavioral approach to treating individuals with borderline personality disorders.
- What is the nature and dimension of the dilemma?
  ○ Dr. Hansen is aware of his lack of supervised experience with working with more directive, empirically supported interventions.
  ○ Recognizing that a rapid referral may be viewed as rejection, Dr. Hansen is unsure of the degree to which he should engage the client in the development of a therapeutic relationship, if unable to competently employ evidence-based interventions.

Generating Potential Courses of Action
- Continue to support the client and engage in a therapeutic contract while monitoring progress toward the agreed-upon goals/outcomes.
- Explain to the client the value of an alternative form of intervention, one for which Dr. Hansen would have to make a referral.
- Employ a dialectical behavioral approach to intervention while seeking ongoing consultation and supervision.

Consulting With a Colleague?
- Rather than connecting with a colleague, Dr. Hansen reviewed the literature in an attempt to find research supporting the effectiveness of a humanistic, nondirective approach to treatment with borderline personality disorders. He also reviewed the diagnostic criteria for the identification of a borderline personality disorder.

Assessing Each Option
- Engaging the client, with strict monitoring of progress, may allow for the initial development of a trusting relationship. However, if progress in achieving the agreed-upon goals of gaining insight about (a) her pattern of failing relationships, (b) the source and impact of her intense fear of abandonment, and (c) the role and "cost" of her engagement in

"risky" sexual behavior is not evident, a referral would have to be made. The challenge might be that with such extended engagement, the client may feel as if the counselor was "giving up" on her.
- Making a referral to an individual competent in working with such a client and client situation appears to be in the best interest of the client, but the client may experience such a referral as rejection and another failed relationship.
- Employing dialectical behavioral therapy with this client would require intense, ongoing supervision. Given the counselor's lack of experience with this form of treatment, the client would genuinely be serving as the "trial run." Even with gaining informed consent from the client, "practicing" on her would not be placing here welfare at the forefront. Therefore, Dr. Hansen felt that this would be self-serving and unethical.

Selecting a Course of Action
- Dr. Hansen concluded that referral to a specialist would be the best option for this client. However, he was aware of the client's abandonment issues. He felt, therefore, that the best course of action would be to engage the client in the development of a strong therapeutic alliance with a focus on assisting client in identifying her goals more clearly. He planned that once this was established to then provide her with information on an alternative approach to the counseling that would most effectively help her achieve these goals.

Implementing a Course of Action
- Dr. Hansen worked with the client for five sessions. He believed that the client felt safe and comfortable with their relationship. During the fifth session, Dr. Hansen was able to highlight the client's long-standing history with broken relationships and her debilitating anxiety around the anticipation of spending her life alone. In this session, Dr. Hansen also raised the issue of some approaches that seemed very useful in helping individuals experiencing such intense fears of abandonment. Upon reflection, he felt the session went well and that the client exhibited an openness to learning more about these new approaches. Thus, he was completely caught off guard when he received a telephone message that said that she "appreciated (his) fine work and all of the help he has provided." She noted that she now felt in a place where she "could move forward on her own" and would not be coming back to therapy. All of Dr. Hansen's attempts to reconnect with this client and engage in follow up failed.

Postscript. Dr. Hansen sought out a consultation on this case to review his decisions and identify possible alternative choices that could have been made. Many what-ifs were identified and alternative possibilities discussed. Following the consult, Dr. Hansen contracted for training and supervision in the use of dialectical behavioral therapy.

Keystones

- Evidence-based practice (EBP) has been defined as "the integration of the best available research with clinical expertise in the context of patient characteristics, culture, and preferences" (APA Presidential Task Force on Evidence-Based Practice, 2006, p. 273).

- Engagement in empirically based practice is more than a practical response to organizational mandates; it also represents adherence to a call for ethical practice. The ACA Code of Ethics states, *"Counselors have a responsibility to the public to engage in counseling practices that are based on rigorous research methodologies"* (ACA, 2014, p. 8).

- Evidence-based treatments, also called empirically supported treatments, have been described as clearly delineated (often manualized) interventions that have produced therapeutic change in controlled trials (Kazdin, 2008).

- Counselors who rely exclusively on their intuition or personal experience as the basis for the formulation of treatment plans also may be violating the ethical directive provided by the ACA that calls for counselors to *"use techniques/procedures/modalities that are grounded in theory and/or have an empirical or scientific foundation"* (ACA, 2014, *Principle* C.7.a, p. 8).

- Given the unfolding science of our profession, the effort to maintain and improve clinical competence is intrinsic to ethical practice for counselors (Jennings et al., 2005). Counselors are ethically responsible to *"maintain their competence in the skills they use, are open to new procedures, and remain informed regarding best practices for working with diverse populations"* (ACA, 2014, Principle C.2.f, p. 9).

- The need for both education and supervision has been codified in the ACA Code of Ethics, which states that counselors engage in a new specialty area or employ a new technique *"only after appropriate education, training, and supervised experience"* (ACA, 2014, Principle C.2.b, p. 8).

- When empirically supported interventions are not identified, counselors can engage in a practice-based evidence model of service, which invites them to systematically collect "information on the process of change and outcome" (Green & Latchford, 2012, p. 87).

Additional Resources

Print-Based

Bertolino, B. (2018). *Effective counseling and psychotherapy: An evidence-based approach.* Springer Publishing.

Brown, C. (2016). *The evidence-based practitioner: Applying research to meet client needs.* F. A. Davis Company.

Dobson, D., & Dobson, K. S. (2016). *Evidence-based practice of cognitive-behavioral therapy* (2nd ed.). Guilford Press.

Williams, L., Patterson, J., & Edwards, T. M. (2014). *Clinician's guide to research methods in family therapy: Foundations of evidence-based practice.* Guilford Press.

Web-Based

American Counseling Association. (2019). Continuing education for counselors. https://www.counseling.org/continuing-education

Society of Clinical Psychology. (2016). Evidence-based treatments. https://www.div12.org/psychological-treatments/

References

American Counseling Association. (2014). *ACA code of ethics.*

American Psychological Association Presidential Task Force on Evidence-Based Practice. (2006). Evidence-based practice in psychology. *American Psychologist, 61,* 271–285.

Baker, S. B. (2012). A new view of evidence-based practice. https://ct.counseling.org/2012/12/a-new-view-of-evidence-based-practice/

Beidas, R. S., & Kendall, P. C. (2010). Training therapists in evidence-based practice: A critical review of studies from a systems-contextual perspective. *Clinical Psychology: Science and Practice, 17,* 1–30.

Bradley, L. J., Sexton, T. L., & Smith, H. B. (2005). The American Counseling Association Practice Research Network (ACA-PRN): A new research tool. *Journal of Counseling & Development, 83,* 488–491.

Carey, J., & Dimmitt, C. (2008). A model for evidence-based elementary school counseling: Using school data, research, and evaluation to enhance practice. *Elementary School Journal, 108,* 422–430.

Chambless, D. L., & Ollendick, T. H. (2001). Empirically supported psychological interventions: Controversies and evidence. *Annual Review of Psychology 52,* 685–716.

Dimmitt, C., Carey, J. C., & Hatch, T. (2007). *Evidence-based school counseling: Making a difference with data-driven practices.* Corwin Press.

Drisko, J. (2017). Active collaboration with clients: An underemphasized but vital part of evidence-based practice. *Social Work, 62*(2), 114–121.

Dunst, C. J., Trivette, C. M., & Cutspec, P. A. (2002). Toward an operational definition of evidence-based practices. *Centerscope, 1*(1), 1–10.

Fairburn, C. G., & Cooper, Z. (2011). Therapist competence, therapy quality, and therapist training. *Behaviour Research and Therapy 49*(6–7), 373–378.

Forman, S. G., Shapiro, E. S., Codding, R. S., Gonzales, J. E., Reddy, L. A., Rosenfield, S. A., & Stoiber, K. C. (2013). Implementation science and school psychology. *School Psychology Quarterly, 28,* 77–100.

Green, D., & Latchford, G. (2012). *Maximising the benefits of psychotherapy: A practice-based evidence approach.* Wiley-Blackwell.

Jennings, L., Sovereign, A., Bottorff, N., Mussell, M. P., & Vye, C. (2005). Nine ethical values of master therapists. *Journal of Mental Health Counseling, 27,* 32–47.

Kazdin, A. E. (2008). Evidence-based treatment and practice: New opportunities to bridge clinical research and practice, enhance the knowledge base, and improve patient care. *American Psychologist, 63,* 146–159.

Margison, F. R., Barkham, M., Evans C., McGrath, G., Clark, J. M., Audin, K., & Connell, J. (2000). Measurement and psychotherapy: Evidence-based practice and practice-based evidence. *The British Journal of Psychiatry 177,* 123–130.

McLaughlin, A. M., Rothery, M., Babins-Wagner, R., & Schleifer, B. (2010). Decision-making and evidence in direct practice. *Clinical Social Work Journal, 38,* 155–163.

Morkides, C. (2009, July). Measuring counselor success. *Counseling Today.* http://ct.counseling.org/2009/07/measuring-counselor-success/

Sackett, D. L., Straus, S. E., Richardson, W. S., Rosenberg, W., & Haynes, R. B. (2000). *Evidence-based medicine: How to practice and teach EBM* (2nd ed.). Churchill Livingstone.

Shimokawa, K., Lambert, M. J., & Smart, D. W. (2010). Enhancing treatment outcome of patients at risk of treatment failure: Meta-analytic and mega-analytic review of a psychotherapy quality assurance system. *Journal of Consulting and Clinical Psychology, 78,* 298–311.

Smith, R. L. (2011). Achievement motivation training: An evidence-based approach to enhancing performance. http://www.counseling.org/resources/library/vistas/2011-v-online/article_56.pdf

Spring, B. (2007). Evidence-based practice in clinical psychology: What it is, why it matters; what you need to know. *Journal of Clinical Psychology, 63*(7), 611–631.

Tarvydas, V., Addy, A., & Fleming, A. (2010). Reconciling evidenced-based research practice with rehabilitation philosophy, ethics, and practice: From dichotomy to dialectic. *Rehabilitation Education, 24,* 191–204.

Weissman, M. M., Verdeli, H., Gameroff, M. J., Bledsoe, S. E., Betts, K., & Mufson, L. (2006). National survey of psychotherapy training in psychiatry, psychology and social work. *Archives of General Psychiatry, 63,* 925–934.

Chapter 10

Conflicts

Ethics and the Law

Is it just me or are these telling me to do two different things?

Throughout this text, you have seen the unique ways counseling ethics and the law can impact a counselor's work in the field. From initiating services to terminating services and everything in between, our professional choices and practices always exist under the umbrella of our legal and ethical obligations. If one thing is clear from the chapters herein, the law and our ethical codes are complicated sets of mandates, and very often they fail to provide an obvious right or wrong answer (Koocher, 2008). This can make the decision-making process extremely complex, whether the issue is an ethical one or a legal one. With that in mind, what happens when the legal decision does not seem to match the ethical one?

This chapter will touch on the issue of conflicts between the law and the professional ethics that guide practitioners in the field. After completing this chapter, readers will be able to

1. identify the nature and purpose of the law in counseling,
2. identify the nature and purpose of counseling ethics,
3. identify circumstances in which the law and counseling ethics may be at odds and why, and
4. explain how to go about attempting to resolving issues in the field when there are conflicts between the law and our ethical codes.

A Force of Nature

On the surface, it may seem counterintuitive that the "right" thing from a legal perspective would not coincide with what is "right" ethically. In fact, the law and our own personal ethics are likely two of the most significant forces that dictate right and wrong in our daily lives. Consider, however, how both change over time. New laws emerge while old laws are struck down or become insufficient for navigating today's complex world. What seems ethical or "right" to us as people today may be significantly different than it was in years past or what it will be in the future. This would seem to indicate that both the law and ethics, whether personal or professional, are ever-evolving and thus, to a certain extent, subjective and open to interpretation. Also consider the fact that although one may characterize the law or ethics as a means to determine right and wrong, their purpose and nature are in fact a bit more complicated. And it is in those subtler nuances that we start to see how laws and ethics can start to conflict.

The Nature of Counseling Ethics and Law

Each professional ethical code has an expressed purpose. It is common that these codes generally serve to inform counseling practices, identify for counselors the common considerations and responsibilities, and serve as a guide for resolving ethical issues (ACA, 2014). As was addressed in Chapter 2, the purpose of individual codes can also vary. Some may be aspirational (e.g., ACA: C.6.e. Contributing to the public good), and others compulsory (e.g., ACA: A.5.a. Sexual and/or romantic relationships prohibited). In either case, all of these codes are anchored in the context of counseling and the role of the counselor.

The nature of the law differs from that of the ethics that guide our practices. The law dictates a set of minimum standards of behavior (Remley & Herlihy, 2016). These laws are most similar to compulsory ethical codes in purpose; however, they obviously dictate behaviors beyond the context of counseling.

The U.S. Constitution serves as the most basic and primary source for the laws that exist today. Specific federal and state statutes may also be a source for laws. The United States also subscribes to English common law. Ahia (2009) defined common law as

> a system of law in which legal principles are derived from usage and custom as expressed by the courts or case law rather than from statutes. A body of legal principles that have evolved and continue to evolve and expand from court decisions. (p. 14)

EXERCISE 10.1

COMMONALITIES ACROSS LAW AND ETHICS

Directions: For this exercise, students are to identify two ethical codes: one aspirational and one compulsory. They are then to research what, if any, laws support or coincide with the identified ethical codes.

Questions for consideration:
- How does the context differ between the code and the law?
- From where does this law originate (e.g., Constitution, state statue)?
- Could context in counseling impact the degree to which these codes and laws coincide?

Put another way, common law is a system whereby court decisions can dictate and define legal principles and standards despite the absence of an explicitly written law. It is here that we can begin to see how otherwise concrete and compulsory descriptions of prescribed behaviors (i.e., laws) can become a source of confusion. Although neither federal and state statutes nor common law principles may contradict the Constitution, federal and state courts are still empowered to *interpret* the law.

Law Versus Ethics

The practice of counseling is evolving. It is continually being shaped by the evolving codes of ethics and emerging laws. The presence of law as a backdrop to our practice can invite counselors not only to feel vulnerable but to act in ways that have as their primary objective the legal safety of the counselor. While litigation is a reality, one that needs to be included in the mix of practice decision making, laws are not meant to make counselors feel threatened. This is most evident when the law parallels and thus further codifies sound ethical practice.

But as noted previously, both ethics and law can often be subject to interpretation. This interpretation can be at the hands of a state, a court, the organizations that create our ethical codes, the boards that govern our licenses to practice, or practitioners themselves. This is an essential component to understanding *how* the law and ethics can seemingly be odds. Very rarely will a practitioner find clear and obvious conflicts between legal mandates and compulsory ethics. Put another way, a practicing counselor is unlikely to run into many issues in which a law mandates they take a certain course of action while their ethical codes clearly forbid it, or vice versa. Where issues are more likely to arise are between interpretations of statutes or common law principles and our ethical codes.

EXERCISE 10.2

REVISITING *TARASOFF*

Directions: Below is a brief summary of the background to the case of Tarasoff vs. the Regents of the University of California (Tarasoff v. Regents of University of California, 17 Cal. 3d 425 (Cal. 1976)). After reading the description you are invited to reflect on the questions posed and discuss with a classmate or colleague.

Prosenjit Poddar was a graduate student attending the University of California, Berkeley. While there, 26-year-old Poddar attended counseling with Dr. Lawrence Moore, a psychologist employed by Berkeley's university counseling center. During the course of this treatment, Poddar revealed to Moore that he intended to kill his girlfriend, Tatiana Tarasoff. In response, Moore moved to have Poddar committed for a psychiatric evaluation. He also notified two campus police officers and sent a letter to the local police chief. Poddar was taken into custody but ultimately released after promising not to contact Tarasoff.

Poddar discontinued services with Moore immediately after his release, and neither Moore nor the police made any attempt to notify Tarasoff of the original threat. Two months later, Poddar stabbed Tarasoff to death on the front porch of her parents' home. Tarasoff's parents successfully sued Moore for not warning her of the original threat against her life.

Questions for consideration:
- What was Moore's professional duty in this case?
    - Ethical duty?
- What was Moore's legal duty in this case?
- What was the source of this legal duty (e.g., constitution, common law)?
- In what way was *interpretation* of law, ethics, or duty a factor in the findings of this case?

In Exercise 10.2, we see clear overlap between our ethical duty to warn and the legal duty to protect potential victims who are both identifiable and in imminent danger. How these ethical and legal duties may seemingly come into conflict is based on how a governing body interprets *the scope* of the practitioner's duty. Perhaps the most well-known example is that of the legal duty to warn in the state of Texas. As stated earlier, court decisions can impact common law principles and how they are applied. These common law principles, however, cannot negate or contradict the law. The reason that the *Tarasoff* rule does not apply in the state of Texas, or at least in the same form seen in other states, is due to the fact that Texas has established its own statute related to exceptions to confidentiality (Tex. Health & Safety Code §611). This statute takes a narrower stance of what qualifies as an exception to confidentiality and, rather than *mandating* a breach, only stipulates that a practitioner *may* breach confidentiality if any of the 11 exceptions are met (Jennings, 2016).

Navigating Legal and Ethical Conflicts

As with all things counseling, prevention is the preferred approach in terms of navigating legal and ethical conflicts. When ethics and law collide, the counselor will need to use a decision-making model that guides them in the direction to take. Needless to say, such a decision must reflect the counselor's accurate understanding of those ethical principles involved, as well as any laws that may be relevant to that decision.

Counselors are urged to continue developing their fluency in the ethics that guide their practice. Just as important, counselors should research the laws of the land and identify their legal duties as well as any potential conflicts that may arise related to specialties, populations of interest, and so on.

Although prevention is preferable, is it not always possible. There may be a situation in which a counselor finds themselves confronted with a decision—one in which the action mandated by law may not appear to be in the best ethical interest of the client. Under such circumstances,

EXERCISE 10.3

LAW OF THE LAND

Directions: For this exercise, students are encouraged to select a state in which they would like to practice upon graduation and review the laws governing each of the following.

- Duty to Warn: Under what conditions must a counselor break confidentiality in response to the duty to warn?
- Privileged Communication: What professions (e.g., Psychiatrist, Licensed Psychologist, Licensed Counselors, etc.) or which specialties (e.g., School Counselors, Drug and Alcohol Rehabilitation Counselors, etc.) are granted Privilege in the state in which you seek to practice? How might that impact your ability to practice?

the counselor needs understanding of all the pertinent information and an ability to discern which avenue both upholds the intent of the law and the essence of the professional code of ethics while providing the maximum benefit to the client.

Throughout this text, you have seen a number of examples of how potential ethical decisions could be made. Resolving the issue of seemingly incompatible legal and ethical mandates is much the same. The counselor must first **identify the problem**. In this process, the counselor should remain focused on the well-being of the client and their role as the counselor. After identifying the problem, the counselor must then **formulate their ethical as well as legal concerns**. This part of the process may be more complicated in cases of ethical and legal conflicts. When identifying concerns, special attention should be paid to the aspirational or compulsory nature of the ethical codes in question, as well as the sources of any potential legal duty (e.g., Constitution, federal/state statute, common law). When identifying these concerns, the counselor should note the extent to which the ethical and legal elements of the issue are open to interpretation.

As with previous examples, the counselor will at this point **generate potential courses of action** and then **consult**. It is important to specify that consultation in such cases may be unique compared to others. Counselors are advised to consult legal counsel with experience in counseling-related issues, as well as colleagues. When consulting colleagues, it may be preferable to identify those with experience practicing in the state and the specific type of system or setting in which the current concern has occurred. Insight into specific interpretations and practices of counselors in that area may prove invaluable. Finally, the counselor will **assess their options and act**. Thorough documentation is advised throughout this process.

Keystones

- Counseling ethics describe a mix of compulsory behavior as well as aspirational best practices.
- The law dictates minimum standards of behavior for all.
- Both ethics and laws are up for interpretation, and those interpretations can happen on a variety of levels.
- It is within the realm of interpretation that most conflicts between ethics and law are bound to emerge.
- Counselors are urged to learn the laws and interpretations of the land in which they practice and make special considerations when resolving potential conflicts.

Additional Resources

Print-Based

Alghazo, R., Upton, T., & Cioe, N. (2011). Duty to warn versus duty to protect confidentiality: Ethical and legal considerations relative to individuals with AIDS/HIV. *Journal of Applied Rehabilitation Counseling, 42*, 43–49.

Paul, R. E. (1977). Tarasoff and the duty to warn: Toward a standard of conduct that balances the rights of clients against the rights of third parties. *Professional Psychology, 8*(2), 125–128.

Wheeler, A. M., & Bertram, B. (2019). *The counselor and the law* (8th ed.). American Counseling Association.

Web-Based

Joe, J. R. (2018). Counseling to end an epidemic: Revisiting the ethics of HIV/AIDS. *Journal of Counseling & Development, 96*, 197–205. https://doi.org/10. 1002/jcad.12192

Stanard, R. & Hazler, R. (1995). Legal and ethical implications of HIV and duty to warn for counselors: Does Tarasoff apply? *Journal of Counseling & Development, 73*, 397–400. https://onlinelibrary.wiley.com/doi/pdf/10.1002/j.1556-6676.1995.tb01771.x

References

Ahia, C. E. (2009). *Legal and ethical dictionary for mental health professionals* (2nd ed.). University Press of America.

American Counseling Association. (2014). *ACA code of ethics*.

Jennings, F. L. (2016). Revisiting the duty to warn issue. *Texas Psychologist, 74*(4), 16–18. https://cdn.ymaws.com/www.texaspsyc.org/resource/collection/9189A1DD-28C9-48D4-9285-8AFC9F0DAE7A/Fall_2016_Texas_Psychologist_Web.pdf

Koocher, G. P. (2008). Ethical challenges in mental health services to children and families. *Journal of Clinical Psychology: In Session, 64*, 1–12.

Remley, T. P., Jr., & Herlihy, B. (2016). *Ethical, legal, and professional issues in counseling* (5th ed.). Pearson.

Tarasoff v. Regents of University of California, 551 P.2d 334 (Cal.Sup.Ct., 1976).

Tex. Health & Safety Code §611.

Index

A
AAMFT Code of Ethics, 96–97, 99, 100
AAMT Code of Ethics, 100
absolutism *vs.* relativism, 16–18
ACA Code of Ethics, 11, 21, 25, 34, 43, 46, 51–52, 111, 114
    boundary violation and, 69
    couples and family counseling, 96
    distance counseling and, 83, 84–85
    Standard B.1.c. of, 59
    Standard B.1.d. of, 60
Ahia, C. E., 15–16, 60, 124
Alliance Defense Fund, 11
American Association for Marriage and Family Therapy (AAMFT), 94
American Counseling Association (ACA), 4. *See also* ACA Code of Ethics
American Counseling Association Practice Research Network, 111
American Personnel and Guidance Association (APGA), 4
American School Counseling Association, 19
animal-assisted therapy, 21
Arredondo, P., 48
Asian Americans, 45
assessment, diverse client population, 46–47
Association for Multicultural Counseling and Development (AMCD) model of multicultural counseling competencies (Arredondo), 48
autonomy, 7, 58–59, 96–97

B
Banks, S., 9
beneficence, 7
Bentham, Jeremy, 6
boundaries, 67–78
    challenges, 73–75
    couples and family counseling, 97–98
    crossing, 70–73
    overview, 67
    proximity, 68
    using ethical decision-making model, 75–78
    violations, 69–70, 70, 72–73

C
case illustration
    boundaries, 69–70
    client and context, 61, 62, 63
    codes of ethics, 8–9, 10–11
    competence, 60
    confidentiality and privacy, 46, 59
    counseling ethics, 17
    couples and families counseling, 98, 100
    distance counseling, 85
    ethical decision making approach, 28–29, 31–32, 32
    evidence-based practice, 110
    experimental design in practice, 115
    Tarasoff v. Regents of the University of California, 10–11
challenges, boundaries, 73–75
Claus, R. E., 25
clients, 57–63
    competence being challenged, 60–61
    consent to services, 60–61
    context and setting, 62–63
    dangerous, 21
    empathic understanding, 48
    legal obligations to protect information of, 59
    mandated, 61
    minors, 58–60
    overview, 57
    verification of, 86
code of ethics, 3–4
    laws and, 10–11
    overview, 3
    practical purpose and use, 9–10
    principles undergirding, 6–9, 7–8
    values and, 5–9
common law, 124–125
communication. *See* privileged communication
competence/competency, 60–61
    couples and family counseling, 94–96
    issue of, 113–114
    multicultural, 48, 49
compulsory codes. *See* obligatory codes
confidentiality, 28–29, 45–46, 58–60, 61, 63, 96, 99–101, 126
consent to services, 60–61
Corey, G., 21, 26
Cottone, R. R., 25
Council for Accreditation of Counseling & Related Educational Programs, 94
counseling relationship and diversity, 45–46
counselor values-based conflict model (CVCM), 33
couples and family counseling, 93–105
    boundaries, 97–98
    competency for, 94–96
    confidentiality, 99–101
    informed consent, 96–97
    overview, 93
    using ethical decision-making model, 101–105
cross-cultural zone, 45
crossing, boundaries, 70–73
culturally sensitive model, 33–37
cultures, 45–46. *See also* diversity

D
dangerous client, 21
Davis, Thomas, 34
deontology *vs.* utilitarianism, 19
diagnosis, diverse client population, 46–47
discretionary ethical codes, 21
distance counseling, 81–91
    ethics and, 84–87
    informed consent and security, 84–87
    interstate practice, 83
    knowledge, 84
    law and, 83
    relationship, 87
    using ethical decision-making model, 88–91
diversity, 43–52
    assessment, 46–47
    challenge to professional assumptions, 44

counseling relationship and, 45–46
diagnosis, 46–47
intervention and treatment planning, 47
multicultural competency, 48, 49
problem identification, 46–47
sensitivity to, 44–47
transcultural approach, 49, 50
using ethical decision-making model, 50–52
Documentation in Counseling Records: An Overview of Ethical, Legal, and Clinical Issues (Mitchell), 36

E
email and texting, 74–75
English common law. *See* common law
The Essentials of Family Therapy (Nichols), 93
ethical bracketing, 33
ethical codes, 19–22
    discretionary, 21
    legal connection, 10–11
    mandatory, 20–21
    multiple, 22
    purpose, 20
    structure, 20
ethical decision making. *See also* models of ethical decision making
    counselor values-based conflict model (CVCM), 33
    culturally sensitive model, 33–37
    integrative model, 29–30, 30
    practice-based models, 26–28, 26–29
    transcultural, 49, 50
    transcultural integrative model, 30–32, 31
ethics
    absolutism *vs.* relativism, 16–18
    conflicts between law and, 123–127
    defined, 15–16
    as definitive mandate, 16
    distance counseling and, 84–87
    law *vs.*, 125–126
    nature of, 124–125
    as philosophy, 16
    principle, 19
    utilitarianism *vs.* deontology, 18–19
evidence-based practice (EBP), 109–111
evidence-based treatments, 111–113

F
familism, 43
fidelity, 8
flexibility, 82
Forester-Miller, Holly, 34

G
Garcia, Jorge, 34

H
Hippocratic oath, 4

I
IAMFC Code of Ethics, 94, 97, 99, 100
identity
    marginalized, 45
    minorities, 44–45
    professional, 22
informed consent, 84–85, 96–97
integrative model, 29–30, 30
International Association of Marriage and Family Counselors (IAMFC), 94, 96, 97, 99, 100
interstate practice, 83
intervention, diverse client population, 47

J
justice, 7

K
Keith-Spiegel, P., 26, 26–27
Kinsella v. Kinsella, 101
knowledge, distance counseling and, 84
Koocher, G. P., 26–27

L
law
    code of ethics and, 10–11
    common, 124–125
    conflicts between ethics and, 123–127
    distance counseling and, 83
    nature of, 124–125
    vs. ethics, 125–126
legal mandates, 10

M
mandated clients, 61
mandatory ethical codes, 20–21
McKelvey, J., 21
medical ethics, 4
minorities, 44–47. *See also* diversity
minors, 58–60. *See also* clients
Mitchell, R. W., 36
models of ethical decision making, 25–38
    boundaries and, 75–78
    counselor values-based conflict model (CVCM), 33
    couples and family counseling and, 101–105
    culturally sensitive model, 33–37
    distance counseling, 88–91
    diversity and, 50–51
    integrative model, 29–30, 30
    practice-based evidence model, 116–118
    practice-based models, 26–28, 26–29
    transcultural integrative model, 30–32, 31
morality, 18
moral principles, 5
Multicultural and Social Justice Counseling Competencies (MSJCC), 48–49
multicultural competency, 48
multiple ethical codes, 22

N
Native Americans, 45
Neukrug, E., 5
Nichols, M. P., 93
nonmaleficence, 7

O
obligatory codes, 20–21. *See also* mandatory ethical codes

P
Percival, Thomas, 4
physicians and Hippocratic oath, 4
Pope, K. S., 20
Port Washington Teachers' Association v. Board of Education of the Port Washington Union Free School District, 63
practice-based evidence model, 114–115
    using ethical decision-making model, 116–118
practice-based models, 26–28, 26–29
principles, 6–9, 7–8, 19
privacy, 45–46, 74, 96, 98

privileged communication, 101
problem identification, diverse client population, 46–47
professional code of ethics. *See* code of ethics
professional identity, 22
prohibitive/restrictive codes. *See also* mandatory ethical codes
proximity boundaries, 68

R
Ratts, M. J., 48, 49
record keeping and access, 99–101
relationship
    distance counseling and, 87
    diversity and, 45–46
relativism *vs.* absolutism, 16–18
restrictive codes. *See* prohibitive/restrictive codes

S
school systems, 62–63
security, distance counseling and, 85–86
Smith, R. L., 113
social media and "friending", 74
social networking site, 74
Society of Clinical Psychology, 111
Steeh, George, 11
Stude, E. W., 21

T
Tarasoff v. Regents of the University of California, 10–11, 125–126
Tavydas, Ruth Ann, 34, 49
texting. *See* email and texting
transcultural ethical decision making, 49, 50
transcultural integrative model, 30–32, 31
treatment
    diverse client population, 47
    evidence-based treatments, 111–113
    psychological, 112

U
U.S. Constitution, 124
utilitarianism *vs.* deontology, 18–19

V
values, 5–9
    to principles, 6–9
Vasquez, M. J. T., 20
veracity, 8
verification of client, 86
violations, boundaries, 69–70, 72–73

W
Ward, Julea, 11
Ward v. Wilbanks, 11
World War II, 4

About the Authors

Richard Parsons, PhD, is a full professor in the Counselor Education Department at West Chester University. Dr. Parsons has over 40 years of clinical experience and university teaching in counselor preparation programs. Dr. Parsons has authored or coauthored over 80 professional articles and books. His most recent books include *Cognitive Therapy: Principles and Practice Applied in Professional and Personal Life* (Cognella Academic Publishing); *The School Counselor as Consultant: Expanding Impact From Intervention to Prevention* (Cognella Academic Publishing); and *Intentional Counseling* (Sage). Dr. Parsons also serves as coeditor for a 24-book series, *Counseling and Professional Identity*, published by Sage Publications, and as editor of a 10-book series, *Guides to Student Success*, published by Cognella Academic Publishing.

Peter J. Boccone, PhD, is an assistant professor in the Counselor Education Department at West Chester University. Dr. Boccone is in his fifth year as a counselor educator, and his primary area of interest is legal and ethical issues in counseling. He has also published/presented on topics related to LGBTQ+ considerations in counseling. Dr. Boccone entered the field as a practitioner in 2006 and is a licensed professional counselor in both Pennsylvania and New Jersey. He is also an approved clinical supervisor.

CPSIA information can be obtained
at www.ICGtesting.com
Printed in the USA
BVHW011141210622
640301BV00003B/29